írish family names

Highlights of 50 Family Histories

ída GREHAN

JB Johnston & Bacon

Johnston & Bacon
Cassell & Collier Macmillan Publishers Ltd., London
35 Red Lion Square, London WC1R 4SG
Sydney, Auckland, Toronto, Johannesburg
The Macmillan Publishing Co. Inc.
New York

First published 1973

ISBN 7179 4840 5

Printed in Great Britain by Butler & Tanner Ltd,
Frome and London

CONTENTS

Barry	1	Hennessy	80
Beirne	4	Kavanagh	83
Blake	6	O'Keeffe	86
Boyle	8	O'Kelly	88
O'Brien	12	O'Kennedy	93
Browne	16	Keogh	95
Burke	20	Lynch	97
Butler	23	MacMahon	101
O'Byrne	26	O'Malley	104
MacCabe	29	Martin	108
MacCarthy	31	Moore	111
O'Connell	34	Murphy	114
O'Connor	37	MacNamara	119
O'Daly	42	O'Neill	121
Dillon	46	Nugent	125
O'Donnell	51	Plunkett	128
O'Donoghue	53	Power	131
O'Donovan	55	O'Reilly	134
Doyle	58	O'Rourke	137
Duffy	61	Sheridan	139
Fitzgerald	63	O'Sullivan	143
O'Flaherty	68	Taaffe	148
O'Grady	71	O'Toole	151
Guinness	74	Walsh	154
Healy	77	Woulfe	158

ACKNOWLEDGEMENTS

The publishers wish to thank the following for the loan of illustrations. By courtesy of the National Gallery of Ireland: 1, 2, 4, 10, 11, 21, 23; 35, 44, 48, 50, 52, 54, 56, 58, 59, 60, 62, 66, 72, 78, 79, 84, 87, 91, 95, 110, 113, 114, 120, 124, 127, 129, 133, 140, 141, 142, 144, 149, 159. The National Library of Ireland: 6, 12, 32, 39, 63, 85, 97, 105, 122, 131, 151. Bord Fáilte: 3, 5, 18, 19, 24, 98, 135, 137, 147. Trinity College, Dublin and The Green Studio, Dublin: Frontispiece, 20, 27. W. G. Field: 9. Shannon Free Airport Development Co.: 15. Austrian Nationalbibliothek: 17, 150. Commissioners of Public Works in Ireland: 30, 69, 102, 152. Muckross House Trustees: 31. Aer Lingus: 37. Irish Times: 41, 70, 76, 92, 94, 100, 156. Arthur Guinness Son & Co., Dublin: 75. Irish Sword: 96, 111, 138, 155. Northern Ireland Tourist Board: 121. Central Press Photos Ltd, London: 136. Ardmore Studios, Bray: 153. Radio Telefís Éireann: 115. Pinakothek, Munich, 117. Miss Nora O'Sullivan, 128. They also wish to thank Miss Myra Maguire, heraldic artist to the Genealogical Office, Dublin Castle, for preparing the coats of arms, pages 161–168.

BIBLIOGRAPHY

Manuscript Sources for the History of Irish Civilisation, Edited by Richard J. Hayes; *Dictionary of National Biography*; *Dictionary of American Biography*; *Compendium of Irish Biography*, Alfred Webb (Gill & Sons, 1878); *Concise Dictionary of Irish Biography*, Dr. John S. Crone (Talbot Press, 1937); *Irish Families, Their Names, Arms and Origins*, Edward MacLysaght; *Surnames and Christian Names in Ireland*, Robert E. Matheson (H.M. Stationery Office, 1901 and 1909); *Irish Names and Surnames*, Father Patrick Woulfe; *The Origin and History of Irish Names of Places*, P. W. Joyce; *The Irish in France*, R. J. Hayes; *A History of Ireland*, Edmund Curtis; *The Gill History of Ireland*; *Dictionary of Irish Writers*, Brian Cleeve; *The Making of Ireland and Its Undoing. 1200–1600*, Alice Stopford Green; *The Norman Invasion of Ireland*, Richard Roche; *The White Seahorse*, (Granuaile O'Malley) Eleanor Fairburn; *King of the Beggars, a life of Daniel O'Connell*, Sean O'Faolain; *Encyclopaedia Britannica*; *Illustrated Ireland Guide*, Bord Failte; *The National Monuments of Ireland*, Bord Failte; *Wonders of Ireland*, Eric Newby and Diana Petry; *Irish Castles*, Harold G. Leask; *Early Christian Ireland*, Maire and Liam de Paor; *The Stranger in Ireland*, Constantia Maxwell; *Burke's Landed Gentry of Ireland, 1958*; *Burke's Peerage, and Baronetage*; *Who's Who*; *The Irish Sword, the magazine of the Military History Society of Ireland*; The journals of the various archaeological, historical and antiquarian societies of Ireland.

PREFACE

WHEN I was asked to compile this book I plunged in with enthusiasm. It is a subject which has always fascinated me—the history of my own people—and it is this interest which has been my inspiration. I could not have attempted it without the constant guidance of Mr. Gerard Slevin, Chief Herald of the Genealogical Office at Dublin Castle. He led me to the source books for my research and kindly read the book in typescript.

Genealogy has always been of great importance to the Irish. We have one of the most ancient recorded lists of pedigrees in Europe. In the seventeenth century the Irish who fled to France were required to prove their noble ancestry with a fully attested pedigree before being granted a commission in the army, or any recognition at court.

Genealogy is history straight. For too long our history has been wrapped in myths. One of the most hopeful signs in Ireland now is that our historians are writing objectively. It is being admitted that although we were colonialized for nearly eight hundred years, the fault was not always entirely our neighbours' that we did not attain independent nationhood.

To follow the fortunes of the foremost families in Ireland, their territorial rivalries, dynastic intermarriages, varying allegiances to church and state, is to see history realistically. Today the captains and the kings have been replaced by the managing directors and the prime ministers. The struggle for power and wealth continues and national boundaries are by-passed by commercial mergers.

In Ireland a long history of emigration has made us aware of the importance of roots. Family means much to us and we can usually name our fourth, if not our fifth cousins, including those in the U.S.A., Canada, Australia, the Argentine etc. Because of our propensity for the losing cause, be it Stuart, Bourbon, Hapsburg or Romanoff, our contacts with Europe have diminished. But now, cost us what it may, we are bounding back into Europe where once before our ancestors held the highest offices.

A brief account of fifty families in Ireland will undoubtedly cause disappointment to at least one hundred and fifty others not included in this book. Each year the small, highly important Genealogical Office in Dublin Castle receives more and more requests for family pedigrees. To help those who would like to pursue their own family history the bibliography contains a list of some of the main sources. Primary personal research should begin with the records of birth, baptism, marriage, death and whatever family papers or verbal accounts can be gathered.

Time puts a limit to the amount of research that can be devoted to each family. I was greatly encouraged by the assistance I received from descendants of many of the families recorded. As well as the help I received from the Genealogical Office, I must thank specifically the staffs of the National Library, the National Gallery, Trinity College, Dublin, the Royal Irish Academy, the Irish Tourist Board, the Board of Works, the Irish Times, my family and many others who helped me discover the facts and the illustrations.

SUMMARY OF MAIN EVENTS
IN IRISH HISTORY

c. 254 AD   Cormac Mac Airt, High King of Tara.

432   St. Patrick arrives in Ireland.

841   The Danes establish a settlement—Dublin—at the mouth of the Liffey.

1002   Brian Boru becomes High King of Ireland.

1014   Brian Boru breaks the Danish power at the Battle of Clontarf (but is himself killed).

1170   Norman invasion of Ireland led by Strongbow (Richard de Clare, Earl of Pembroke).

1366   The Statutes of Kilkenny enacted to stop the Gaelicization of the Anglo-Normans.

1394   Richard II of England lands in Ireland with a large army.

1399   Richard II again visits Ireland.

1487   Lambert Simnel, the Pretender, crowned as Edward VI of England in Christ Church Cathedral, Dublin.

1494   Poynings' Law, subjecting the Irish Parliament to English Privy Council, enacted at Drogheda.

1534   The rebellion of Silken Thomas Fitzgerald crushed by English forces.

1536   Anglo-Irish parliament acknowledges Henry VIII of England as King (instead of Lord) of Ireland, and head of the Church of Ireland. Suppression of monasteries follows.

1591   Foundation of Trinity College, Dublin.

1594   Hugh O'Neill's nine years' war against the English begins.

1598   The English defeated by O'Neill in the Battle of the Yellow Ford, Armagh.

1602   Spanish forces, and Irish under O'Neill and O'Donnell, defeated at Kinsale under Lord Deputy Mountjoy.

1607   The 'Flight of the Earls' (O'Neill and O'Donnell) opens the way for the Plantation of Ulster with Protestant settlers.

1641   Ulster Rising against Protestant settlers commences and quickly spreads to other parts of Ireland.

1646   Eoghan Rua O'Neill defeats the English at Benburb, County Tyrone.

1649–1650   Cromwell subdues Ireland.

1689   James II lands in Ireland after losing the throne of England to William of Orange.

1690   James II's forces defeated by William's at the Battle of the Boyne.

1691   The Jacobites finally capitulate and the Treaty of Limerick is signed. Their departure to France follows (the Flight of the Wild Geese).

1695–1727 Penal Laws enacted against the Catholic population in violation of the Treaty of Limerick.

1782 England acknowledges the independence of the Dublin Parliament.

1798 Nationwide insurrection planned by United Irishmen breaks out, but is gradually suppressed. Lord Edward Fitzgerald dies of wounds after arrest. Wolfe Tone imprisoned and executed.

1800 Act of Union with Great Britain; end of separate parliament.

1803 Robert Emmet's abortive insurrection.

1829 Daniel O'Connell wins Catholic Emancipation.

1846–1847 The failure of the potato crop causes the Great Famine. Population reduced by death and emigration from 8 m to 4 m.

1848 The Young Irelanders make an abortive attempt at insurrection.

1858 The Irish Republican Brotherhood (Fenian Movement) is founded by exiles in America.

1869 Isaac Butt founds the Home Rule Party, leadership of which Charles Stewart Parnell assumes four years later.

1885 Gladstone's first Home Rule Bill defeated in British House of Commons.

1890 Downfall of Parnell. He dies the next year.

1893 Gaelic League founded by Doctor Douglas Hyde.

1905 Sinn Fein movement founded by Arthur Griffith.

1912 Irish Home Rule Bill passed by British House of Commons is due to come into effect in 1914, but its provisions are defied by the 'Ulster Volunteers'. Bill suspended for duration of the Great War.

1916 Easter Week Rising. Proclamation of Irish Republic. Insurrection crushed after four days.

1919 Fighting breaks out again between Irish and British forces.

1921 Treaty with Britain establishing Irish Free State of 26 counties. Civil War between Free-Staters and Republicans follows.

1926 Republicans led by De Valera form Fianna Fail party.

1932 Fianna Fail party comes to power. International Eucharistic Congress held in Dublin.

1937 New Constitution adopted by plebiscite, declaring Ireland to be 'a sovereign independent democratic state'.

1938 Douglas Hyde elected first President of Ireland.

1949 Government repeal External Relations Act, 1936, and provide that description of the State shall be Republic of Ireland. British Government state they regard this step as placing Ireland outside the Commonwealth.

1955 Ireland enters U.N. December 15.

1973 Ireland becomes member of E.E.C.

(By permission of the Bord Failte)

Script taken from early Irish genealogies originally compiled in the tenth century. This copy was written in the first half of the fourteenth century by Lucas Ó Dalláin, a scribe of one of the learned Irish families, and is reproduced from a manuscript in Trinity College, Dublin

BARRY

THE Norman conquest of Ireland, which began in May 1169, was almost a family affair. The FitzStephens, FitzHenrys and FitzGeralds who spearheaded the adventure were kinsmen, all grandsons of Nesta, 'the Helen of Wales', a daughter of Thys ap Tewdwr Mawr who was the last independent prince of south Wales. From her many paramours, including Henry I, she had numerous children who, named after their sires, were the FitzStephens, FitzHenrys and FitzGeralds—the latter to become one of the most numerous, most distinguished and enduring Irish families.

With her husband, William de Barri, a Norman nobleman, Nesta had three sons, Robert and Philip who were with the first Irish invaders, and Gerald, a cleric educated in Paris who, following his brothers in their Irish adventure, arrived there first in 1183 as court chaplain. He became the unique chronicler of the Norman conquest and has since been known as Giraldus Cambrensis (1147–1223). His *Topography of Ireland* and his *Conquest of Ireland*, written in Latin, are the contemporary account of this turning point in Irish history. Although he saw it only from his Welsh-Norman point of view and had no feeling whatever for the invaded Irish who, not unnaturally, resisted fiercely, his chronicles remain a most valuable historical source.

Of the three grandsons of Nesta of Wales, only Philip de Barri settled in

James Barry (1667–1747), 4th Earl of Barrymore, descendant of Philip de Barri

Ireland. He was granted extensive lands in County Cork where he established the Barry dynasty. In succeeding generations they scattered over Ireland while some went to France or to the Americas.

Buttevant, where the Barrys settled in County Cork, derived its name from

1

the family motto, *'Boutez en avant'*, which means 'Strike forward' and was their battle cry. An Augustinian abbey near Buttevant was founded by Philip de Barri and the castle where Spenser wrote *The Faerie Queen* is nearby.

David Fitzjames de Barry, Viscount Buttevant (1550–1617), was with the Irish and the Geraldines in the rebellion of 1579–1583. Sir Walter Raleigh, a neighbour, wrote of him, 'David Barry has burnt all his castles and gone into rebellion.' However, when the English captured his brother he returned to the royalist side and had the forfeited lands of the MacCarthys bestowed on him by King James.

Gerat or Gerald Barry (fl. 1624–1642) was of the family of which the Earls of Barrymore and Viscounts Buttevant were the leaders. He entered the Spanish army at an early age and distinguished himself at the siege of Breda in 1625. For a period he returned to fight in Ireland in the 1641 uprising but he was too old for their guerilla tactics. He is best remembered as a military historian and particularly for his *Discourse on Military Discipline* which was found useful by the Spanish king, Philip IV.

'Lo', probably Lording Barry (born c. 1591), is thought to be the first of the recognized Irish dramatists. He wrote and produced his *Ram Alley* in London about 1610.

Spranger Barry (1719–1777), an actor-manager, divided his talents between Dublin, Cork and London. His superb figure and voice were outstanding. He played Shakespeare with, and later against, the great Garrick—with whom he had developed a corrosive rivalry.

James Barry (1741–1806) left Dublin to become a celebrated London painter. He was befriended by Edmund Burke who financed his studies in Italy. Like his kinsman, Spranger Barry, he had a violently quarrelsome nature which eventually caused his expulsion from the Royal Academy.

John Barry of Wexford (1745–1803) who was said to have been 'bred to the

Spranger Barry (1719–1777), the actor and contemporary of Garrick

The statue at Wexford town of Commodore John Barry (1745–1803)

sea', emigrated to Philadelphia and had a remarkable naval career. He has been called the 'Father of the American navy'. In Ireland he has been honoured with a postage stamp, and a statue commemorates him at Wexford harbour.

Physicians were numerous in the family. Sir Edward Barry (1696–1776) was President of the King and Queen's College of Physicians in Ireland, and was elected to the Irish House of Commons.

To John Milner Barry (1768–1822) Ireland owes the benefit of vaccination. He introduced it to Cork in 1800.

Many of the Barrys followed legal careers. Sir Redmond Barry (1813–1880), went to New South Wales to become a judge and first Chancellor of the new university of Melbourne. Its public library and Technological Institution, and the National Gallery at Victoria, are testimony to the vitality of this lawyer originally from County Cork.

Another Redmond, the Right Honourable Redmond Barry, was Lord Chancellor of Ireland from 1911–1913. His son, Sir Patrick Barry, who died in 1972, was a judge of the Queen's Bench Division in London's High Court. He presided over many notorious cases, including the trial of Colin Jordan and the Vassal spy case.

The antecedents of Alfred Étienne Edward Barry fled from Ireland to France at the end of the seventeenth century, just before the decisive Battle of the Boyne. A learned professor of history at the Lycée du Lyon, he later held the Chair of History at La Faculté des Lettres de Toulouse and spent many years working on his universal history.

Patrick Barry, born in 1816 in Belfast, emigrated to America and became a pioneer fruit grower in New York.

Kevin Barry, a Dublin medical student who was hanged for his part in the 1916 rising, is a folk hero.

Tom Barry who led the West Cork Brigade in the War of Independence wrote his story *Guerilla Days in Ireland*. At Crossbarry with one hundred and four men he dispersed five thousand British troops.

Philip Barry, born in Rochester, New York, of Irish parentage, in 1896, wrote *The Philadelphia Story*, a successful play, starring Katherine Hepburn.

3

BEIRNE

WITH or without the O prefix, the Beirnes are an important sept of North Connacht. Although the name may appear to be similar, they are not to be confused with the O'Byrnes. Their coats of arms are quite different. That of the O'Beirnes is unusually picturesque: a fruit tree has a green lizard at its base while overhead there is a full sun and a crescent moon, demonstrating how Irish heraldry makes particular use of natural things.

The Beirnes were not confined to the West where they originated from, and they particularly distinguished themselves in the Midlands in the eighteenth century. Two brothers, born at Farnagh, County Longford, were both sent to St. Omer in France by their wealthy farmer father to study for the priesthood. Their careers were rather different from what he could have anticipated. John Beirne became a parish priest, while Thomas Lewis Beirne, born in 1748, became

Thomas Lewis Beirne (1748–1823), churchman and writer

4

Clifden, County Galway—O'Beirne country

a parson. Both ministered for a while in the same County Meath parish.
Thomas was continually writing controversial tracts. In his early days he went
to England and was appointed Chaplain of the Fleet under Lord Howe. On a
visit to New York he is recorded as giving a most vigorous sermon at St. Paul's
Church. He lived for a long while in England where he enthusiastically supported
the Whigs. He also wrote for the theatre and was taken up by high society. He
acted as Chaplain and as Private Secretary to the Duke of Portland, a Viceroy
of Ireland. Although Thomas Beirne had many rich chaplaincies in England he
preferred to end his days as Bishop of Meath where he was regarded by his flock
as an admirable prelate. One of his original ideas was the uniting of the church
of England and Ireland. His appearance was described as 'striking', for he had
'a penetrating glance and long, flowing white hair'. During his Meath episcopacy
he built fifty-seven churches and seventy-two glebe houses and he died there in
1823 at Lee House, Ardbraccan.

Eugene Francis O'Beirne, although no relation of Thomas Beirne's also had
a different attitude towards matters clerical. He has left a succinct and,
seemingly, accurate account of 'the system of discipline of Maynooth College,
containing an account of the system of tyranny pursued therein'. This was
published in Dublin in 1835.

In the eighteenth century when so many Irishman had to flee abroad the
O'Beirnes were distinguished in the service of France.

An Irish emigrant, Henry O'Beirne, born in 1851, was a popular writer in
America. He wrote vividly about the Texas Indians with whom he lived for the
remainder of his days.

BLAKE

CADDELL was the original surname of the family who some time between their leaving Wales and becoming a prominent Galway tribe, changed their name to Blake. Perhaps Robert Caddell, 'le Blaca', who is said to have come to Galway in 1277, fits the description 'the black'.

At Carnmore, formerly Ballimacroe, County Galway, the Blake family lived

Sir Valentine Blake, Mayor of Galway from 1634 to 1644

almost uninterruptedly for nearly six centuries.

There were, of course, many branches of this family. For centuries a Blake was Mayor, Sheriff or Burgess of the 'City of the Tribes'. Robert Blake was Mayor of Galway around 1624 when, 'for the first time freemen of the town were made capable to vote'. He has also gone down in records as the first Mayor for thirty years not questioned for recusancy, which suggests he must have

6

accepted the Reformation. Not so his son, John. As Sheriff of Galway, he was deprived of this dignity by Cromwell's Commissioners for being an Irish Papist.

Nor did all the Blakes keep to the role of Galway merchants. James joined the military and with the rank of captain went, in 1591, to solicit the King of Spain to invade Galway. After the defeat of the Irish and their Spanish allies at Kinsale in 1601, James entered the service of the English and, it is said, was sent by Sir George Carew into Spain to poison the tragic Red Hugh O'Donnell who had fled there after the Kinsale defeat. Red Hugh died in Simancas in 1602 in very suspicious circumstances.

The marriage records of the Blakes show them intermarrying almost exclusively with the other Galway tribes, with the Lynches, Kirwans, Brownes, Frenchs. James, for instance, had married Margery, daughter of Dominick Browne, reputed to be 'the richest merchant in Ireland'.

The church of St. Nicholas in Galway city where there is a tradition that Columbus prayed before sailing to discover America, is still a fine example of Norman-Irish architecture. It was particularly dear to the Blakes. An heiress daughter, Cilly Blake, in 1438 made over her inheritance to keep up the perpetual grants made to it by her family.

The Blakes have been well documented. In *The Blake Family Records, 1600–1700* compiled by Martin J. Blake, there is a portrait of Sir Valentine Blake of Menlo, Mayor of Galway from 1634–1644. Menlo is now a romantic ruin by the waters of the Corrib at Galway. The house was accidentally burned down about the turn of the century.

Sir Francis Blake, the son of a political writer, was himself a mathematician. He seems to have emigrated to Canada about 1728.

Sir Henry Arthur Blake, born at Limerick in 1840, followed the line of so many of the Irish landed gentry—he became Governor of a string of British colonies; the Bahamas, Newfoundland, Jamaica, Hong Kong and Ceylon. Using the name 'Terence McGrath' he wrote about his travels abroad and also *Pictures from Ireland.* He died at Youghal in 1918.

England's Poet-Laureate who died in 1972, Cecil Day-Lewis, born in 1904 in Ballintubber, County Leix, was brought up by his aunt, a Blake of Galway. Appropriately, he chose 'Nicholas Blake' as the pen-name of his many successful detective novels.

A popular American actor of his day, William Rufus Blake, 1805–1863, was of Galway parentage.

Martin Joseph Blake, 1853–1931, did extensive genealogical research into the Blake family who were big landowners in Connacht in the sixteenth century, where they had houses and castles at Ardfry, Ballyglunin, Kiltullagh, Menlo and Renvyle.

Some Blakes branched out into Mayo. There were O'Brien-ffrench-Blakes there at Kilnock. Gradually, they crop up in other counties. William Hare Blake, born in 1809 in Kiltegan, County Wicklow, died in Toronto, Canada, in 1832 where he had practised at the Canadian Bar and had become Solicitor General and Chancellor of Upper Canada.

There were Blakes in County Kildare. The town of Blakeston is named after them. There were also Blakes in the West of Ireland of earlier, Gaelic origin. Their name in Irish was O Blachmhaich which was anglicized to Blowick, or more commonly, Blake.

BOYLE

A S it was in ancient times and is still today, Donegal is the country of the Gaelic-Irish Boyles. From Ballyweel (in Irish 'the home of the O'Boyles'), until the break-up of the old Gaelic order in the mid-seventeenth century, they shared the leadership of the north-west with those other formidable chieftains, the O'Donnells and O'Doughtertys.

The Boyles of Desart, Armagh, are a very ancient family from the Barony of Boylagh, County Donegal who, according to *Burke's Landed Gentry*, settled some two hundred years ago and had great possessions in County Derry.

The Boyles at Limavady, County Derry, have been there since 1660. Alicia Boyle (b.1908), the painter, is one of these. She is represented in the permanent collections of Northampton Art Gallery and the Belfast City Art Gallery.

In the *Dictionary of National Biography* fifteen Boyles are written about extensively. Of these, fourteen descend from the same Boyle ancestor who came originally from England. This was Richard Boyle (1566–1643), who set out to make his fortune in Ireland and did so. In 1588, with £27 3s. 0d., a diamond ring, a bracelet, a few clothes and a very sound education, he arrived in Munster and in a comparatively short time acquired a large proportion of it. The precursor of modern developers he became a medieval millionaire and was ennobled as the First Earl of Cork. He married twice and each time very well. When Sir Walter Raleigh fell from grace and was executed Richard Boyle bought up his vast County Cork estates for the paltry sum of £1,000. He also bought cheaply abbey lands and Fitzgerald properties, and built the town of Bandon, having ousted from the area the O'Mahonys, O'Donovans, O'Driscolls, O'Learys and other native septs, and planted his estates with English and Scottish settlers.

A man far ahead of his time, Richard Boyle introduced ironworks, built bridges, harbours, towns and thirteen strong castles. Everywhere he brought in English settlers to pursue the mechanical arts and manufactures. It was said of him, 'If there had been one like him in every province it would have been impossible for the Irish to raise a rebellion.' He commanded eight votes in the Irish House of Commons and it was said that his brother, Michael Boyle, born in London, was appointed Bishop of Waterford and Lismore, and that a cousin became Archbishop of Tuam, 'through the interest and pecuniary assistance of Richard Boyle, First Earl of Cork'.

However, he did have some difficulties over his too astute financial deals. Sir Thomas Strafford (1593–1641), Lord Lieutenant of Ireland, was no friend of his. In his efforts to increase Charles I's rent and tithes, he made Richard Boyle surrender the college of Youghal which he had taken from the Earl of Desmond and he fined him £15,000 for various flaws and evasions of the law. But Strafford had made many enemies and he was impeached and beheaded by the Long Parliament in 1641, a very important date in Irish history for it marked the beginning of the end of the government of the Irish by the Irish as the new colonialists began to take over by force. Richard Boyle died a few years later and the monument he arranged to be built to commemorate himself, his two

The tomb in St. Mary's Collegiate Church, Youghal, erected in memory of Richard Boyle and his family

wives and the achievements of his fourteen children still stands, a trifle decayed, in the cathedral of Youghal, not far from the former home of Sir Walter Raleigh.

The Boyle children were all exceptionally talented. The girls married noblemen and the boys acquired titles, with one remarkable exception. He was the seventh son and fourteenth child, Robert (1627–1691) who is regarded as being the earliest chemist and the inventor of Boyle's Law—the discovery of the

9

elasticity of air. Despite what he described as 'a lifelong torturing malady, bad eyes and a treacherous memory', he was a brilliant natural philosopher and 'a linguist by necessity'. At the time of Galileo, because of the strife in Ireland, he went to Florence to pursue his studies. Later he came to England where, at his own expense, he printed bibles in the Irish, Indian and Welsh languages. He played a leading role in the founding of Britain's Royal Society. He was a most religious man and for this reason he declined all the honours and titles that were offered him.

Richard Boyle (1621–1679), third of the seven sons of Richard Boyle of Cork, was elevated to the peerage as Baron of Broghill at the age of seven. He grew

Robert Boyle (1627–1691), early chemist and inventor of Boyle's Law

up to be a remarkably versatile statesman and general. First he fought on Cromwell's side, then he changed his allegiance to Charles II who, after proclaiming himself king in Dublin on 14th May, 1660, gave power and honours to former Cromwellian leaders, including Richard Boyle who was created 1st Earl of Orrery. From his wide experience in both Ireland and England he later wrote his celebrated *Treatises on the Art of War*.

A great-grandson of Richard Boyle, 1st Earl of Cork, was another Richard, the 3rd Earl of Burlington (1695–1753), who began the rage for Palladian architecture in England. He reconstructed Burlington House, of which the poet Gay said, 'Beauty within; without, proportion reigns.' Lord Hervey, however,

Henry Boyle, Earl of Shannon (1682–1764)

said of this London landmark, 'Possessed of one great hall of state, without a room to sleep or eat.' So intent was Richard on his architectural embellishing he ran out of money and had to sell his Irish estates to pay his English debts.

Henry, Earl of Shannon (1682–1764), born at Castlemartyr, County Cork, was also a direct descendant of the 1st Earl of Cork. His mother, Lady Mary O'Brien, was the daughter of Murrough O'Brien, 1st Earl of Inchiquin and President of Munster. In 1729 this Henry Boyle distinguished himself in parliament in Dublin by successfully resisting an attempt by the government to obtain a vote for a continuation of supplies to the crown for twenty-one years. Sir Robert Walpole is said to have called him the 'King of the Irish Commons'. A highly competent and conscientious administrator, he held high offices as Chancellor of the Exchequer, Commissioner for Revenue in Ireland and Speaker of the House of Commons. In 1753 he became very popular with the people because he opposed the government proposal for appropriating a surplus in the Irish exchequer, but this caused his dismissal from offices held under the Crown.

In more recent times there was Richard Vicars Boyle, an engineer, born in Dublin in 1822, whose profession was constructing railroads. He travelled continually in India where, during the Mutiny, he defended his house with only fifty men against three thousand rebels. For five years he was Engineer-in-Chief of the railways in Japan.

John Boyle, journalist and self-styled poet laureate, who died in 1832, is remembered as a wit, and William Boyle (1853–1922), was one of the earliest dramatists to contribute to Dublin's Abbey Theatre. He was a civil servant and was born in Dromiskin, County Louth. His best known play is probably *The Eloquent Dempsey* which was put on at the Abbey Theatre in 1905.

11

O'BRIEN

B RIAN BORU (926–1014), High King of Munster for thirty-eight years, came nearer than any man yet to uniting Ireland. By dividing Ireland between himself and Malachy the High King, they consistently drove away the marauding Vikings. He also rebuilt the ruined monasteries and sent overseas to replace their lost books. He is credited with originating surnames although they did not become common until long after his death. Brian seems also to

Brian Boru (926–1014), High King of Ireland

have limited royal succession to male heirs, a factor which has deprived Irish history of a certain balance.

Perhaps he may have been influenced by Gormflath, one of the women, rare in Irish history, so characterful they stand out like beacons. An Irish Cleopatra, she was beautiful and power-hungry. She became wife, first to the Norseman Olaf, then to the High King Malachy. When Malachy repudiated her she turned to Brian. Ambitious to put Sitric, her son by Olaf, in power, it was her scheming—she offered him her hand—which brought Sigurd, Earl of Orkney, and his Irish and Scottish allies to do battle in Dublin Bay on Good Friday, 23rd April, 1014. There, Brian's forces won the most resounding of all Irish

12

victories, the Battle of Clontarf. Too venerable for activity, Brian watched unguarded in his tent, and was slain by an escaping Norseman. Sigurd, too, and many of his allies were killed. Gormflath is heard of no more, but Donough, her son by Brian, began the lineage of the O'Briens who, with the O'Neills and the O'Connors were for many centuries the leading aristocratic families of the Gael.

The sept which began with Brian and his son Donough divided into many branches. The O'Brien possessions included the whole of County Clare and large tracts of the counties of Limerick, Tipperary and Waterford.

Brian's son, Donough, far from building on the foundations laid by his great father, occupied himself with warring and plundering and savage disputes over chieftaincy succession. This pattern continued for several centuries; relatives suspected of having designs on a kingship were liable to be put to death, or to have their eyes gouged out. Depending on what suited their thirst for power, or for revenge on a neighbouring chieftain, they fought with or against the English. A medieval chronicler described the chiefs who waged these tribal wars as being 'capable of sudden rallies and the accomplishments of brilliant exploits but quite incapable of sustained or combined efforts of any kind'. They had often to make a humiliating submission to the English monarchy.

In 1540 there was a coalition of O'Brien, O'Neill, O'Connor and O'Donnell, but it came to nothing. It was at this point that Henry VIII, backed by considerable power, began to assert his claim to be king of all Ireland. The notorious Murrough O'Brien, later the 1st Baron of Inchiquin, showed his realism by offering his support to Henry if his estates were confirmed to him. At that time the concept of nationalism had not been greatly developed. Murrough was loaned £100 so that he could visit London, where Henry VIII created him 1st Earl of Thomond in 1543.

Donough O'Brien, the 4th Earl of Thomond (d.1624), a Governor of Clare and Thomond, lies buried in Limerick Cathedral. 'The Great Earl', a son of Conor O'Brien (1534–1580), he was one of those Irish heirs cunningly brought up at the court of Queen Elizabeth with the intention of winning them away from their insurgent kinsmen in Ireland. In 1599, at the head of a numerous army of Queen's troops, he visited his Irish domains and found them ravaged, whereupon he inflicted terrible retaliation, hanging the garrison of the castle of Dunbeg in couples on the nearest trees.

Many legends are related in County Clare of the fiery Máire Ruadh, a tough red-headed MacMahon married to Conor O'Brien. Together, in 1643, they rebuilt the fine castle of Leamaneh near Kilfenora in County Clare. In 1651 Conor was mortally wounded in battle against the Cromwellian General Ludlow. Maire is said to have refused to take her husband into the house as she wanted no dead man to help in its defence. However, she relented and he died within it. To save her son's estate from seizure she subsequently married a Cromwellian cornet of horse, whom, according to the legend, she disposed of by kicking him in the stomach. Leamaneh remains, a splendid ruin.

As the Penal Laws made life increasingly difficult, the landed gentry began to move to Europe, taking with them their families and retainers. The 3rd Viscount Clare, Daniel O'Brien (d.1690) raised the Irish Brigade regiment known as Clare's Dragoons which was later commanded in many famous European battles by a Marshal of France, Charles O'Brien, 5th Viscount Clare, who was killed at Ramillies in 1706.

13

With the approach of the eighteenth century the O'Brien castles and towers had become a feature of County Limerick, Clare and Tipperary. The O'Briens themselves, at home and abroad, were now statesmen, rather than swordsmen. Sir Lucius O'Brien (d.1794), descended from a younger son of the first Baron Inchiquin, was M.P. for Clare and a Privy Councillor to whose opinions the House of Commons paid a deference only partly due to his 'illustrious lineage'.

Lucius was the grandfather of William Smith O'Brien (1803–1864) who was born at Dromoland Castle, County Clare. At first William followed the aristocratic land-owning pattern; Harrow, Cambridge, M.P. for Ennis, Conservative. Gradually he developed nationalist views and veered wholeheartedly towards the Young Irelanders who wanted to see the Union with Britain repealed. Daniel O'Connell, the Liberator who won Catholic emancipation, said of him, 'He now occupies his natural position, the position which centuries ago was occupied by his ancestor, Brian Boru.' Smith O'Brien became a leader of the Young Irelanders and in 1848, he and other landowners took to arms in a dismal attempt at revolt. They hoped for aid from France but this was not forthcoming as the monarchy fell that year.

Following State trials Smith O'Brien and the other leaders spent some years of imprisonment in Australia. He was pardoned in 1854 and it was he who, in his last speech in the British House of Commons, the very day of the great Chartist demonstrations led by another O'Brien, James Bronterre, warned that if his country 'were not allowed her own legislature they would have to encounter the chance of a republic in Ireland'—prophetic words a century ahead of their becoming fact!

The numerous O'Briens are one of the most colourful of the Dalcassian families. They have contributed to every facet of Irish life. Since earliest Christian times they have been churchmen and bishops. Terence Albert O'Brien (1600–1651) had his head struck off by Ireton at Limerick. James Thomas O'Brien, Bishop of Ossory, Ferns and Leighlin (1792–1874), was said to 'possess perhaps the loftiest and best cultured intellect that Dublin University has produced since the time of Bishop Berkeley' (the philosopher). Despite his opposition to the disestablishment of the Church of Ireland, when this was accomplished he was one of its main reorganizers.

The O'Brien military ventures were more conclusive abroad than at home. Captain Jeremiah O'Brien and his brothers John and William struck the first blow at sea in the naval battles of the American War of Independence. The Irish author and exile, Fitzjames O'Brien (1828–1862), volunteered for the northern army in the Civil War and died from a wound.

In more recent times the O'Briens who come to the fore are from all over Ireland and are not predominantly of the aristocracy. An exception, Charlotte Grace O'Brien (1845–1909) was a daughter of William Smith O'Brien. She had been moved by the conditions she had seen on the 'coffin ships' in which the Irish emigrants went to America and she did much philanthropic work on their behalf. She wrote books and became an ardent member of the Gaelic League for the restoration of the Irish language.

Dillon O'Brien of Roscommon, who had gone to America after the famine of 1846, described the life of the Irish emigrants of that time in his novels of American life.

Kate O'Brien (1897), born in Limerick, has written many plays and novels.

Interior of the restored Bunratty Castle, former stronghold of the O'Briens

In 1931, *Without My Cloak*, her book about small-town Irish life, won the Hawthornden Prize, and less than enthusiasm from County Limerick. She has lived in, and written about Spain, and during her most fruitful years she suffered the distinction of leading writers of that time—the banning of her books by the Irish Censorship Board.

Conor Cruise O'Brien (1917), began a versatile career as a civil servant in the Department of External Affairs. In 1955/56 he was Counsellor in Paris, Head of the United Nations Section and a member of the Irish Delegation to the United Nations. In 1961 he was a representative of the Secretary General of the U.N. in Katanga. He resigned from the Irish Civil Service and, during the premiership of Nkrumah was, for a while, Chancellor of Ghana University. He returned from a university post in New York to join the Irish Labour party and to become a Minister in its Coalition government which came to power in 1973.

Edna O'Brien (1932), is the convent girl from County Clare who went to Dublin, married briefly, moved to England and wrote *The Country Girls*, a sensationally simple novel which became an immediate success. It has been followed by many others.

In Ireland, Vincent O'Brien is synonymous with the turf, horses and The Curragh, County Kildare, where he trains some of the finest race horses competing on international courses.

Two of the show places in Clare are former strongholds of the O'Briens of Thomond, Inchiquin and Clare. Dromoland Castle is a hotel and Bunratty Castle, fully restored, is the scene of regular medieval dinners. In its folk park there are samples of every type of Irish dwelling.

BROWNE

ALTHOUGH Brown may not be essentially a Gaelic name, it is a very common surname in Ireland, particularly with an E. The Brownes were one of the celebrated 'Tribes of Galway', and Browne is the family name of a host of Anglo-Irish and Anglo-Norman nobility. Le Brun of Normandy was an ancestor of the Brownes of Galway. Sir Nicholas Browne, an Elizabethan settler, was given great estates in Kerry and from him descended the Earls of Kenmare, only recently extinct. There are Brownes of Breaghy in County Mayo, and Browne is the family name of the present and 10th Marquess of Sligo, and of Lord Oranmore and Browne, the 4th Baron.

These Norman Brownes of Galway intermarried with prominent Irish families; the Lynches, O'Flahertys, O'Malleys, Blakes. By no means did they confine their alliances to fellow members of 'The Tribes'.

With or without the final E, the Brownes were distinguished churchmen of the differing Christian denominations. Ignatius Brown, born in Waterford, was a Jesuit, a cosmopolitan and a writer. At one time he was rector of the Irish seminary at Poitiers. He had been educated in Spain and was confessor to the Queen of Spain. He died in 1679.

Bishop Peter Browne, was Dublin born and held the diverse ecclesiastical posts of Provost of Trinity College, Dublin, and Bishop of Cork. He was also remarkable for his pronouncements on metaphysics though he is best remembered for a sermon he gave against the practice of drinking over zealously to the deceased. He died in Cork in 1735.

More recently Ireland has had a Cardinal Browne. Michael David Browne, born in 1887 in County Tipperary, was a learned Dominican who held many distinguished appointments in the Vatican.

Monsignor Patrick Browne of Tipperary, who died some years ago, was President of University College, Galway, and a major scholar and Gaelic poet. Michael Browne, of Westport and Bishop of Galway, has left his mark on that ancient city because of the imposing cathedral he master-minded.

A recitation of the vicissitudes of Irish families will inevitably include a list of those driven out by one or other of the two dynamic social factors—politics and religion. The Brownes, although not reckoned to be true Gaels, were no exception. George Browne (1698–1792), was born at Camus, County Limerick, of a Catholic and Jacobite family. A soldier of fortune, he offered his sword to the Russian army in 1730. He was three times imprisoned and was sold as a slave to the Turks. After many adventures he was released and he showed such skill and bravery he was appointed a Field Marshal by Peter III. As Count George Browne he was later Governor of Livonia and he was such a favourite with the Empress Catherine she would not consent to lose his services, so he remained in Russia until he died at the age of ninety-four.

A relative of his (also from Camus), Maximilian Ulysses Browne (1705–1757), whose father was an Irish exile after the Battle of the Boyne in 1690, entered the imperial service of Austria and became a Field Marshal. He was made a Count of the Empire by Charles VI.

16

Maximilian Ulysses Browne, Field Marshal in the Austrian army

Perhaps the most famous of all the Irish Browns is William Brown (1777–1857) who was born in Foxford, County Mayo. He worked his way up from cabin boy in the American Mercantile Marine to the command of a merchant vessel from which he was induced to enter the Argentine navy. Under his command it defeated two Spanish squadrons and the Brazilian fleet. During the civil war of 1842–1845 he blockaded Monte Video. Admiral William Brown ended his days in Buenos Aires.

The Irish Browns frequently combined learning with travelling. Patrick Browne (1720–1790) of Woodstock, County Mayo, was a naturalist who took his medical degree in Leyden and became a friend of the great Linnaeus. He travelled widely and published a *History of Jamaica*, and catalogues of the birds, fishes, etc. of his native country.

Andrew Brown, born in the north of Ireland in 1744, was educated at Trinity College, Dublin, and saw service in America as an officer in the British army. He settled in Massachusetts and fought on the American side at Lexington and Bunker Hill. When peace was established he attempted to set up an academy for young ladies in Philadelphia but had not the temperament required to make a success of it. Instead he took to publishing and was successful with his *Philadelphia Gazette* in which he was the first to regularly report debates in Congress.

Another family of Brownes who made their contribution to the United States were descended from the Reverend Arthur Browne who was born in Drogheda in 1699, nine years after the fateful Battle of the Boyne. Obviously not a Jacobite, he played a full part in Irish life, becoming a Vicar General of the Diocese of Kildare and he was returned to the Irish House of Commons. It was his son, Arthur, who went to America where he was rector of Trinity Church, Rhode Island. *His* son, a third Arthur, must have returned for a while to Ireland for he was educated at Trinity College, Dublin, where he studied for the Bar. He was one of the original fellows of Rhode Island College which, from 1804, has been known as Browne University.

In 1784, Sir William Brown of Ballymena went to Baltimore where he prospered in the linen trade. Later he re-crossed the Atlantic to open a branch of his business in Liverpool where he played a prominent part in the civic life of South Lancashire. He was a Member of Parliament, Chairman of the Atlantic Telegraph Company, and he erected the free library and Derby Museum in Liverpool.

During the year 1793 when there were great fears in Ireland of an invasion by France, a Mr. Browne, the Parliamentary representative for Mayo, attributed the local unrest 'to the new political doctrines which have pervaded the lower classes', and he went on to say, 'This spirit has been produced by the circulation of Paine's *Rights of Man*, of seditious newspapers, and by the shopkeepers who, having been in Dublin to buy goods have formed connections with some of the United Irishmen.' Mr. Browne was convinced that if there were to be a landing

Colonel John Browne and his wife, painted by Kneller

of French troops, 'they would be joined by the peasantry of Connaught'. He was, in fact, anticipating Wolfe Tone's abortive landing in 1796.

A journalist, John Ross Browne, born in 1822, went abroad at an early age. At first he had little success with his writing or his travelling, so he shipped before the mast on a whaler bound for the Indian Ocean. This gave him material for his *Etchings on a Whaling Cruise*. A serious traveller, he toured Europe and the East, settling eventually in Oakland, California, where he reared a large family. He wrote for *Harper's Magazine*, and in 1869 was so well thought of he was sent for two years as U.S. Minister to China.

The only Brown lady to achieve fame was a very remarkable person indeed. She was Frances Brown, the blind poetess of Donegal. Born there in 1816, she educated herself by hearing others doing their lessons. She wrote poems and published volumes of verse and novels and was granted a civil list pension. She died in London in 1879.

In the literary world of the twentieth century an outstanding character is Christy Brown who burst into print with *My Left Foot*, his autobiography. Almost completely paralysed from birth, his mother taught him to read, and to write—which he did, with his left foot. Born in the slums of Dublin in 1932 he has achieved maturity and international acclaim with his novel *Down All The Days*.

18

Westport House, County Mayo

Garech Browne (born 1939) is a member of the Connacht Oranmore and Browne family. An ancestor of his, Dominick Browne, one of the many Brownes who were M.P.s and Mayors of Galway, had his knighthood conferred on him in 1635 by the Lord Deputy, Sir Thomas Wentworth. These Galway Brownes were dispossessed of their lands by Cromwell, but, after the Restoration, they were mostly restored and the family were active in the Irish army of James II. Garech Browne has contributed substantially to the greater understanding and appreciation of Irish folk music and ballads by encouraging exchanges with other Celtic poets and musicians and by the making of recordings.

Westport House in County Mayo is one of the show places of Ireland. A fine Georgian mansion it stands on the site of an ancient castle of the O'Malleys (the dungeons are still to be seen, and visited). It commands a magnificent view over Clew Bay and the Atlantic Ocean, to Achill and Clare Island and Ireland's Holy Mountain, Croagh Patrick. The original house was built by Colonel John Browne and his wife, ancestors of the present Marquess of Sligo. He was a Jacobite who was at the siege of Limerick; she was a great great grand-daughter of Grace O'Malley, the sea-faring pirate queen of Connacht in Elizabeth's time.

The house has a fine collection of old silver and a library with many old Irish books and manuscripts. There are portraits by Sir Joshua Reynolds of the 1st Earl of Altamont, and of the Rt. Hon. Denis Browne, brother of the 1st Marquess and a member of Grattan's Parliament. Beechy did the portrait of the 2nd Marquess who spent four months in an English jail for bribing British seamen in time of war to bring his ship, full of antiquities, from Greece to Westport. This same Marquess was a friend of George IV and of the poet Byron. Westport House, which was built by the famous Robert Castels and completed by James Wyatt, also has a most splendid collection of paintings of the locality by James O'Connor, now regarded most highly as an Irish landscape painter.

Lord Altamont, son of the present Marquess, has opened the family home and its treasures to the public. He has established an art gallery, an antique shop and other numerous temptations—a veritable shopping complex beneath a stately home, and close to the village of Westport.

BURKE

THE Irish poets, whose job it was to take care of public relations for the families to whom they were attached, put it around that the Burkes were Franks, descended from Charlemagne. There are many Burkes and who is to say that some of them did not come to Ireland via Aachen?

The name has a number of variations; Burke, Bourke or the Norman de Burgo or Burgh, and it is generally accepted that William Fitzadelm de Burgo, he who was called William the Conqueror by the Irish annalists, was the original of the Burkes.

de Burgo knight, reproduced from a genealogical manuscript in the library of Trinity College, Dublin

Irish women, with few exceptions, however nobly born, were shadows in the background, essentially for consolidating land deals and producing sons. The Normans shrewdly married Irish princesses. William de Burgo married an O'Brien and so acquired the noble blood of the great Brian Boru which flowed on through Mortimers and York and James II to the present British royal family. A de Burgo married Strongbow's heiress daughter, Isabella, in 1189. Walter, son of William, became Lord of Connacht in 1264, and began a de Burgo dynasty which lasted until 1333.

For years the Anglo-Normans who ruled Galway City—the twelve tribes—forbade its Gaelic neighbours to enter it. This applied particularly to the Burkes, the O'Flahertys and the O'Malleys. At the same time there was lamentable enmity between the Burkes and the O'Flahertys. Yet there was also intermarriage. Grania O'Malley, the pirate queen and one of the outstanding women of medieval times, an O'Flaherty widow, married secondly Richard Burke.

In the first confiscation of Connacht around 1565, another branch of the sept, led by Richard de Burgo, drove out the O'Flahertys, a deed remembered in Oughterard to this present day. Ulick Burke of Galway, submitted to Henry VIII

Edmund Burke, philosopher, statesman and orator

who made him 1st Earl of Clanrickard around 1577. He had a great house with an underground passage to the port and it was an ancestor of his, another Richard de Burgo (he died in 1243) who is credited with having built the original town of Galway.

Grania O'Malley had three sons, two O'Flahertys and a Burke who became Viscount Sir Theobald Burke and fought on the English side at the battle of Kinsale. After that tragic Irish defeat many families fled to the service of France and Spain, and this also included some of the Burkes.

Fighting was by no means the only attribute of this powerful family. There were two de Burgo bishops of Clonfert in the sixteenth century.

Edmund Burke, born in Dublin in 1729, earned international renown as philosopher, statesman and orator of the highest rank. He advocated many unpopular causes; the Americans; the Catholics; Irish Trade. He became a Tory M.P., and he deplored the excesses of the French Revolution.

Sir Richard Burke, also Dublin born in 1777, claimed kinship with the great Edmund and, assisted by Earl Fitzwilliam, edited Burke's correspondence. Sir Richard was also a Major-General and colonial governor of the Cape and of New South Wales.

One of the first of the Irish revivalists, most influential through his teachings and writings, was Canon Ulick Bourke. Born in County Galway in 1829, the statesman Arthur Griffith said of him, 'In his circumstances and those of his time few men could have done more for the Irish language.' He was Parish Priest of Claremorris at his death in 1887.

Walter Hussey Burgh, yet another statesman and orator, was born in Kildare in 1742 and died in Armagh. He studied law at Dublin's Trinity College and it was said of him, 'No modern speaker approaches him in power of stirring the passions.' Contemporary with Walter, there was also William of Kilkenny, a politician and controversialist. He went to live in England where he advocated the abolition of the slave trade and opposed the Union. To York Minster he bequeathed his library.

The Burkes filled many roles; sometimes met violent deaths. Thomas Henry Burke, a Galway man and an Under Secretary at Dublin Castle, was killed by 'Invincibles' in the Phoenix Park, Dublin, in 1882. Richard Southwell Bourke, 6th Earl of Mayo, a statesman, was, 'one of the ablest administrators that ever ruled India'. He was assassinated while visiting penal settlements in the Andaman Islands.

Robert O'Hara Burke of St. Cleran's, Galway, was an explorer, a captain in the Austrian army, an inspector of police in Australia. With W. J. Wills, he was the first white man to cross that continent from North to South. They both died from starvation on the return journey in 1861.

William Burke from Cork was hanged as a criminal. With his fellow country-man, Hare, he inveigled strangers into his Edinburgh lodging house, made them drunk, suffocated them and sold their bodies for dissection. His awful deeds added a new verb, 'to burke', to the English language.

Research for this and many another book has been aided by the lasting work left by John Burke and his son, Sir John Bernard Burke, a genealogist from Tipperary who, in the last century, compiled many books on the peerage, the landed gentry and Irish families. Sir John, who died in 1892, was Ulster King of Arms at Dublin Castle.

In medieval times, to distinguish one Burke from another, they might place a Mac before their first name. Thus were MacWilliam, MacDavies, MacGibbon, MacHugo, MacRedmond and MacSeoinin originally of the Burke family. Today a Burke could be traced from a Gibbons, or a MacSeoinin anglicized to Jennings: and the de Burgo patronymic still lingers on in ancient families who can trace their lineage to the Norman invasion, back to William Fitzadelm de Burgo.

It is one of the most numerous of the Hiberno-Norman surnames and is fourteenth in the list of the commonest Irish names.

BUTLER

THE founder of the Butler family, Theobald Fitzwalter, came to Ireland in 1171. His younger brother, Thomas, landed with Prince, later King, John of England, at Waterford in 1185. They acquired land in Limerick, Tipperary and Wicklow, building castles and abbeys until Butler fortresses guarded every river and pass from Arklow to County Clare.

Henry II appointed Theobald Chief Butler in Ireland, a hereditary title which the family still hold. Some Butlers became Gaelic in culture and adopted Gaelic names. As the family branched out they acquired different titles. They took part in many dreary feuds. It is said the Norman Butlers who favoured the English did so because they were not so given to fighting as the Fitzgeralds. From the Norman conquest till long after the Battle of the Boyne no other family

James, 1st Duke of Ormonde (1610–1688)

in Ireland produced such a succession of able administrators, churchmen and soldiers.

James, the 1st Earl of Ormonde, who was born at Kilkenny in 1331, was called 'The noble Earl' because he was related to both Edward I and Edward III of England.

James, the 3rd Earl, built Gowran Castle and later bought the castle of Kilkenny which was to be the home of the Butlers until the 1920's.

Sir Piers Butler, the 8th Earl, from whose family the poet W. B. Yeats is descended, was induced by Henry VIII to surrender the Ormonde title in favour

The tomb of Piers Rua Butler and his wife, who was daughter of Garret Mor Fitzgerald, in St. Canice's Cathedral, Kilkenny

of Sir Thomas Boleyn, his relative by marriage and father of the ill-fated Anne Boleyn, who was to become the mother of Queen Elizabeth I of England. Sir Piers received large grants of land for suppressing the Fitzgeralds. It was Sir Piers who brought workmen from Flanders and other parts of Europe to embellish the splendid castle at Kilkenny. Today, the castle and the grounds are preserved, but it is in the magnificent stables that the interest lies. Here the Kilkenny Design Workshops have been established to stimulate and promote Irish design.

Black Tom, the 10th Earl, born in 1532, was brought up in the court of Henry VIII. His mother, a Fitzgerald heiress, was the famous Countess of Desmond who lived for well over a hundred years. Queen Elizabeth is said to have had a soft spot for her distant cousin, Black Tom. It is even supposed she bore him a son—Piers Butler of Duiske. For her he built the Tudor manor-house at

24

Carrick-on-Suir, though Elizabeth never honoured her Black Tom with a visit there. The house has been restored and is open to the public.

Three Butlers were Archbishops. One of them, Edmund, a natural son of Piers the 8th Earl, was educated at Oxford and became Prior of Athassel Abbey, County Tipperary. He had been Archbishop of Cashel for thirteen years when he was deposed by Thomas Cromwell in 1537.

In the seventeenth century the Butlers began to travel abroad. Count Walter, born at Roscrea, was a soldier of fortune who served with the German army for thirty years. He is credited with having discovered Wallenstein's treachery and to have arranged his assassination, in return for which he was rewarded with large estates in Bohemia, where he died at Schondorf in 1633.

Ireland owes its Public Record Office and its Genealogical Office to the inspiration of the Butlers. To the Ormondes must also go the credit for Dublin's splendid Phoenix Park. During one of his terms as Viceroy, James Butler, the great Duke of Ormonde, a loyalist at the time of Charles I and II, created the Phoenix Park. He is said to have been the most brilliant of the Ormondes and that if he had done more to win the sympathy of the native Irish, the course of Irish history would have been considerably happier.

In sharp contrast to that Earl of Ormonde was the Pierce Butler who was present at the siege of Derry, the battles at the Boyne and Aughrim. He was one of those who had to sign the notorious Treaty of Limerick. He could have saved his own estates but he preferred to follow Patrick Sarsfield to France where he, too, achieved distinction as a brigadier in the Irish Brigade. He died in 1740 in France.

In the next generation another Pierce Butler left Ireland to settle in California where he became an American statesman and senator. He died in 1822.

One of the Butler ladies achieved unusual notoriety. She was Lady Eleanor, sister of the 17th Earl of Ormonde, who, with her friend, Sarah Ponsonby, lived in eccentric seclusion in Wales where they were renowned as 'The Ladies of Llangollen'.

The Honourable Simon Butler, born in Dublin in 1757, was the first President of the Society of United Irishmen and a distinguished lawyer. He directed the Society from Scotland when he had to flee the country.

Richard Butler went to America to serve in the American army and he died there in 1777.

Another Richard, the Reverend Richard Butler, was a poet, philosopher and a friend of Wordsworth. He returned to Ireland to become Vicar of Trim where, during the famine, his efforts were said to be untiring. He wrote a history of Trim, County Meath.

Sir William Francis Butler, born in Tipperary in 1838, was a soldier and eventually an author. He served in the British army in many African campaigns but resigned his command because he sympathized with the Boers.

The thirty-first Chief Butler and 25th Earl and 7th Marquess of Ormonde, Charles Butler, lives in Illinois, U.S.A.

There are estimated to be about nine thousand Butlers in Ireland. They are very well documented and there is a Butler Society at Kilkenny which produces a regular bulletin and keeps in touch with Butler branches in various parts of the world. In 1967 they held a great gathering at Kilkenny where Butlers came from England, from Russia, Poland, Spain and other parts of Europe. In Hesse a yearly gathering is organized by the German branch of the family.

BYRNE (O'Byrne)

T HE O'Byrne surname (in Irish it is O'Broin) is derived from Bran (meaning the raven), son of Maolmórdha, King of Leinster, who is recorded as having died in Cologne in the year 1052. Byrne, less frequently with its O' prefix, is most common in Leinster and has spread into the four provinces in Ireland.

Originally the O'Byrne patrimony was in north County Kildare, until they were driven out by the Anglo-Normans when they sought refuge in the nearby Wicklow Mountains. Here the O'Byrnes became very powerful and for three hundred years waged continuous guerilla warfare on the invaders with no really decisive victory on either side.

In 1580 when Fiach MacHugh succeeded to the O'Byrne chieftancy he joined forces with Lord Baltinglass (James Eustace) and they defeated the English Lord Grey in an engagement at Glenmalure. It was a short-lived victory and Fiach MacHugh retreated to his headquarters at Ballinacor, from which he conducted forays against the foreigners inside the Pale or those he considered his natural enemies. At one time he did submit formally in Christ Church, Dublin, but, as was suspected, it was a mere formality.

When Red Hugh O'Donnell and Art O'Neill, the young sons of Sir Hugh O'Donnell, Chief of Tirconnell, and Shane O'Neill, escaped from their long imprisonment in Dublin Castle at Christmas 1591, it was to Ballinacor, across the snowy Wicklow Mountains, they made their painful way. Young Art O'Neill died from exposure, but the O'Byrnes led O'Donnell safely home to Fermanagh.

Rose O'Toole, a sister of the O'Toole chieftain of Castlekevin, was the second wife of Fiach MacHugh O'Byrne. Though women infrequently appear in the chronicles, Rose O'Toole must have been a woman of standing. At one time when Fiach could not be present at a parley held by the great Hugh O'Neill, he wrote to ask if she could represent Fiach. He also arranged for her safe conduct. In the Leabhar Branach, the book of the O'Byrnes, the poets are unusually fulsome in their praise of her beauty and wisdom.

In 1597 Fiach MacHugh O'Byrne was finally captured by the forces of the Queen's Lord Deputy. His head was cut off and impaled on the gates of Dublin Castle.

His son, Phelim, was confirmed as his successor by patent of Queen Elizabeth I. Because of the perjury common to the courtly adventurers of those times, although the charges trumped up against him were disproved, he was deprived of his inheritance and the Wicklow O'Byrnes lost nearly all their possessions. In 1628, Phelim O'Byrne, Chief of the O'Byrnes, it is reported, 'was turned out upon the world a beggar'.

He was by no means the only Irishman to be thrown upon the mercy of the world in those harsh times. There was another O'Byrne, Daniel Byrne of Slane and Timogue in the Queen's County (Leix), who was not too proud to turn his hand to trade when dispossessed of his estates. He went into the tailoring business, making uniforms because he felt the army at least would pay regularly. He did very well, so splendidly that his son Gregory was made a baronet in May 1671. The story is told that as father and son were walking together in Dublin, Sir Gregory said: 'Father, you ought to walk on the left of me, I being

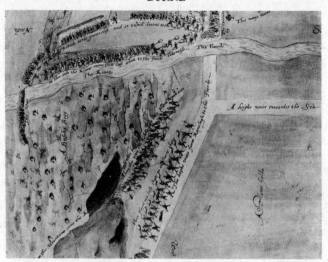

Part of a map painted on vellum entitled 'Sir Henry Harrington's defeat in the Berne's countrie (Byrne country) neere unto Wickloe'—probably one of Fiach MacHugh O'Byrne's many forays. (Reproduced from a manuscript in the library of Trinity College, Dublin)

a Knight and you but a private individual.' 'No, you puppy,' said Daniel, 'I have the precedency in three ways. Firstly, I am your senior; secondly, I am your father; and thirdly, I am the son of a gentleman and you are but the son of a poor lousy tailor.'

Gregory's descendants married profitably into the English and French aristocracy.

There was a celebrated Byrne, not of the nobility, who made a fortune in a rare way, though briefly. This was Charles Byrne (1761–1783) known the length of Britain as the Irish Giant. His father was Irish; his mother Scottish. Both were normal physically but their son was eight feet four inches tall. He travelled about the country exhibiting himself at shows. In London in 1783 he created a sensation in a pantomime at the Haymarket, *Harlequin Teague or the Giant's Causeway*. But he died, a youth of twenty, from 'drink and vexation at losing £750 at Cockspur Street, Charing Cross'. His skeleton is in the Museum of the College of Surgeons in Lincoln's Inn, London.

A number of the O'Byrnes, because of their adherence to the Stuart cause, had to flee from Ireland. They went mostly to France. Among the leading Irish citizens recorded at Bordeaux were Gregory, Daniel, John and Emily O'Byrne, formerly of Cabinteely, County Dublin, and probably descendants of 'Daniel the Tailor'. Gregory was a Captain in Berwick's Irish Regiment. During the French Revolution the Abbé O'Byrne was imprisoned in Luxembourg. Madame Florence O'Byrne, a Royalist, mother of three sons who were adherents of the Vendean insurgents, was guillotined. Patrick James O'Byrne, Doctor of the Sorbonne, Superior of the Irish College in Paris, escaped to Ireland to become President of Maynooth College. John O'Byrne fought in the 92nd Regiment of the revolutionary army—the former Regiment of Walsh.

27

Miles Byrne (1780–1862), son of a Wexford farmer, in 1796 agreed to join the hated yeomanry on condition that he would obtain the renewal of the lease on his mother's land. However, because of his brother's death, he was absolved from serving and thus, 'never wore a red coat'. Instead, he carried a pike and fought at Vinegar Hill in 1798 with the United Irishmen. He was sent by Robert Emmet to Paris to Robert's brother, Thomas Addis Emmet, the agent there of the United Irishmen. From Bordeaux he sent a report on the state of Ireland to Napoleon who, in 1803, decreed the formation of the Irish Legion in the service of France. Because of the collapse of Emmet's conspiracy, Miles Byrne remained in France where he was commissioned and served in Napoleon's campaigns. After the Revolution of 1830 he received the cross of the Legion of Honour from Louis Philippe. He held strong views on freedom and his Memoirs in three volumes were published in Paris in 1863. There is a monument to him in Montmartre.

William Richard O'Byrne (1823–1896) was the author of *The Naval Biography* 1849–1854, a work so valuable he was given a substantial testimonial from the Board of the Admiralty and from a thousand naval officers. He was High Sheriff of Wicklow and a Home Rule M.P. for County Wicklow. He succeeded to the family estates at Cabinteely, County Dublin, which, because of land depreciation, were of little value to him.

Andrew Byrne (1802–1862), born in Navan, County Meath, ended his days in America as Bishop of Little Rock. He was ordained in Charleston, North Carolina and was sent home to Ireland on two occasions to try to recruit nuns and priests for his mission. At home, for a while, he became involved in politics and preached on the repeal of the Union.

John Byrne (1825–1902) was a pioneer in electric surgery. His study of physics led to his ingenious adaptation of the electric cautery knife to surgery. Following studies at home and in Britain, he practised in Ireland during the Famine before emigrating to New York where he graduated again from the New York Medical College.

Brian Oswald Donn-Byrne (1889–1928), the novelist, was born in New York County of parents temporarily resident there from Forkhill, County Armagh. They returned home and he spent his childhood in the Glens of Antrim. He studied at University College, Dublin, and, through the influence of Doctor Douglas Hyde, the folklorist and founder of the Gaelic League, he became interested in Irish history and literature. In Paris and Leipzig he studied for a diplomatic career, but abandoned it when he fell in love with an Irish girl whom he followed to New York and married in 1911. He had hopes of being a serious Irish poet, but was forced te accept less congenial employment in New York, contributing to encyclopaedias and dictionaries. The poet, Joyce Kilmer, helped him to return to serious writing and he produced a series of novels which had immense vogue in their day. *Messer Marco Polo* is probably his best known novel. At the early age of thirty-nine he was killed in a motor accident in Ireland and a headstone under a quicken tree at Rathclaren, near Kilbrittain, County Cork, commemorates this Irish-American novelist.

One of the best loved Lord Mayors of Dublin was Alderman Alfred Byrne (1882–1956). A Dubliner born, he reared most of his family in the Lord Mayor's handsome house in Dawson Street during the ten years preceding the second world war when he was Lord Mayor of Dublin.

MacCABE

THE Scottish gallowglasses were first-rate fighting men. In medieval Ireland few chieftains would consider themselves secure without their protection and until the sixteenth century they formed the strong arm of Irish warfare. The gallowglasses came from the Hebrides, Inis Gall—the Isles of the Norsemen—and it was from there the MacCabes came as Captains of gallowglasses to the O'Rourkes and the O'Reillys of Breffny, now known as Leitrim and Cavan. It is thought they may be a branch of the Scottish MacLeods and they are frequently mentioned in the Annals of the Four Masters. Today they are a most numerous family, and MacCabes are still to be found mostly in that northwest area of Ireland.

Cathaoir MacCabe who was born in Mullagh in Cavan was a very popular bard. His great friend, the blind Turlough O'Carolan (1670–1738), the most famous of Irish harpers, was not only a musician but also a composer and poet. When O'Carolan died, Cathaoir wrote a most beautiful lament. Strangely enough, Turlough O'Carolan had himself once written an elegy for Cathaoir MacCabe having been hoaxed into believing him dead. He survived O'Carolan by only two years and some of his manuscripts are preserved in the British Museum Library.

William Putnam MacCabe is probably the best recorded of all the MacCabes. His father, Thomas, was a watchmaker and part owner of a cotton mill. It was Thomas MacCabe who was largely responsible for stopping the Belfast merchants from fitting out their ships for the lucrative slave trade. William, who was born in Belfast in 1776, is supposed to have been one of Lord Edward Fitzgerald's bodyguards. He had a useful knack of eluding the law by his aptitude for disguise and mimicry. A gentleman in Wexford who knew him well and met him on many different occasions has testified that he could never recognize William until he revealed his identity. He was a member of the United Irishmen during the 1798 rising. He was captured but he managed to persuade the Scots soldiers who guarded him that he was their fellow country-man. Thinking they had wrongly arrested him, he was released. However, with Lord Edward dead and the United Irishmen defeated, there was no future for him in Ireland, so he went to France where, following his father's trade, he established a cotton mill near Rouen. He died in Paris at the early age of forty-five.

The MacCabes have had the distinction of a cardinal in the family. Edward Cardinal MacCabe was born in Dublin in 1816 and was educated at Maynooth College. As parish priest of Dun Laoghaire, County Dublin, he built the parish church there which was burned accidentally in the 1960's. Essentially a towns-man, he was regarded as out of sympathy with the land agitation which was troubling the country during his time.

The American protestant bishop known during the Civil War as 'Chaplain MacCabe' (1836–1906) was Charles Caldwell MacCabe. He was the grandson of a County Tyrone MacCabe and he died in America.

Many historical romances came from the pen of William Bernard MacCabe, a Dublin journalist who died at Donnybrook in 1861. *Agnes Arnold* was probably his best known work.

Farm management was the career chosen by Eugene MacCabe, born in 1930 in Kildare. He combined it most successfully with playwriting when *King of the Castle* was proclaimed the major success of the Dublin Theatre Festival of 1954.

The MacCabes came from the Hebrides to Ireland as captains of gallowglasses. These figures, from a tomb in Roscommon Abbey, show (left) a mercenary soldier and (right) a gallowglass, a first-rate fighting man

MacCARTHY

OF all the Irish Mac names, MacCarthy is the most numerous, especially around Tipperary, Cork and Kerry. Not only is it an ancient name, but also an eminent one, for it is chronicled often in the Annals of the Four Masters. It was Cormac MacCarthy, son of Muiredach, King of Munster, who, around 1130, erected on the magnificent Rock of Cashel what is known to this day as Cormac's Chapel. Donal Roe MacCarthy, Prince of Desmond from 1244, was buried there and when his tomb was opened a century ago, in it was found the ancient Crozier of Lismore. It is now in the National Museum in Dublin. The British Museum has probably one of the few existing charters of an Irish King, that of Dermod, son of Cormac MacCarthy.

These princely MacCarthys built splendid castles all over their Munster territories; Muckross, Macroom, Killaha, Mourne, Timoleague, Srugrena, Kanturk and many more.

About 1446 Cormac MacCarthy built Blarney Castle. Another Cormac, a descendant, gave the English language a new word for eloquence—'Blarney'. Although he fought with the English against the local Fitzgeralds—there is a letter from Henry VIII 'on the State of Ireland' which is supposed to have been addressed to him—Cormac struggled to preserve his own independence. It seems he also put off Queen Elizabeth's demands for his allegiance 'with fair words and soft speech—pleasant talk intended to deceive without offending'. This is how the Blarney Stone acquired its world-wide reputation for imparting eloquence to those who succeed in kissing it!

Blarney Castle, seat of the MacCarthys

Donald MacCarthy Mor, of the senior branch of the family, was created Earl of Clancare and Baron of Valentia by Queen Elizabeth. He lived at a critical time in Irish history when the old Gaelic order was beginning to break up. Like most of the nobility, the MacCarthys were engaged in continuous struggles for place and power, with their neighbours, and with invaders.

Although little has come down to us of their women, a Lady Eleanor is remembered because she protected Garrett Fitzgerald after the murder of his five uncles by Henry VIII in 1537. Another MacCarthy lady who became involved in the power struggle with English royalty was the Lady Ellen, daughter and sole heiress of Donal MacCarthy Mor. Despite the difficulties of communication between Cork and London in medieval days, the MacCarthys had close contact with Queen Elizabeth who looked upon their rich lands as her own. Florence (Fineen) MacCarthy Reagh, chieftain and son of Sir Donagh MacCarthy Reagh, Lord of Carbery in Munster, was graciously received and rewarded by Elizabeth

Romantic midnight marriage of Florence MacCarthy Reagh and Lady Aileen Mac-Carthy Mor at Muckross Abbey, Killarney

for serving the Crown against the Fitzgeralds of Desmond. Nationalism was not then known. However, Florence gave great offence by secretly marrying the Lady Ellen, his kinswoman, at a midnight ceremony in Muckross Abbey. Suspecting this union of the two main branches of the Clan Carthy to be a threat to her Munster sovereignty, the Queen committed him to the Tower of London. For this she worked up a treason charge—conniving with the Spanish was included—and Florence was in and out of the Tower for the next thirty-seven years. He died in 1640.

He has been described as a man of heroic stature and benignant aspect. Fortunately, he was also a scholar, and in his intervals in the Tower he wrote a history of Ireland though it had to wait until 1858 for publication. Fruitless years were spent in wrangling over his Irish properties, and alas, for the romantic midnight marriage! In his later years he had little affection for the Lady Ellen who had borne him four sons.

From the twelfth to the sixteenth century the MacCarthys ruled as chieftains of Desmond, i.e. South Munster. The titles bestowed on them by Elizabeth were forfeited for their part in the Jacobite war. As soldiers, the MacCarthys had plenty to engage them in Ireland until they were finally driven out to put their military prowess to use in Europe, Africa and America.

Justin MacCarthy, Viscount Mountcashel, was well known in the court of Louis XIV of France.

Charles, of the house of Muskerry, commanded a regiment in the service of the King of Portugal and became Governor of Miranda.

Governing came naturally to the MacCarthys. Sir Charles MacCarthy, a well-esteemed Governor of the Gold Coast who took up the cause of slavery, also became involved in the Ashanti war and was killed in 1824. Perhaps he is remembered by MacCarthy's Island, off the West African coast?

In the eighteenth century a MacCarthy was Governor of Madras and in the nineteenth Sir Charles Justin MacCarthy was Governor of Ceylon.

In France the MacCarthys distinguished themselves in the army and in the church. Nicholas Tuite MacCarthy who died in 1833 at Annecy, was regarded in France as one of the most magnificent of preachers.

Justin, Count MacCarthy of Tipperary who settled at Toulouse, was renowned for his library which was said to have been worthy of a sovereign.

Among those who stayed in Ireland, John George MacCarthy, who died in Cork in 1892, was a land commissioner and an author who believed in peasant proprietorship, rare for that time.

The great poet of the MacCarthys was Denis Florence MacCarthy who died in 1882. He was Dublin born and there he held the chair of English literature and poetry in the Catholic University of Ireland. For his translations of Spanish literature, he was awarded a medal of the Royal Academy of Spain.

J. J. MacCarthy who designed St. Patrick's Catholic Church in Armagh has been described as the Irish Pugin.

It was not until 1896 that a MacCarthy was beatified. This was Blessed Thaddeus MacCarthy, Bishop of Cork and Cloyne, who died in 1492 in France after a long struggle against political intrigue.

A junior branch of the MacCarthy Mor family has been traced to Montreal. There have been numerous MacCarthys in America. Colonel Daniel E. MacCarthy was the first American soldier to set foot in France in 1917. A. H. MacCarthy was a prominent American mountaineer. Governor C. J. MacCarthy was President of the Pan Pacific Union at the beginning of this century. Munster could possibly also lay claim to nurturing the antecedents of Senator Joseph MacCarthy, the American investigator of Communism, and, perhaps, the novelist, Mary MacCarthy?

In the service of the United Nations, with the Irish Defence Forces in the Middle East, Colonel Justin MacCarthy was killed a few years ago.

In war and marriage the MacCarthys have been allied to most of the great Irish families. The beautiful Muckross estate of MacCarthy Mor at Killarney is now in the care of the State and is a splendid centre for the history and folk arts of Kerry. It is in a rarely beautiful setting by the Lakes of Killarney, close to the Abbey where Florence secretly married his kinswoman.

O'CONNELL

O'CONNELL is one of the most numerous names in Ireland, its origins going back to before the time of Christ. The Irish surname came from the descendants of Conall, a powerful ancient Irish chieftain. There are other versions of Connall. In Welsh it is Cynvall, the British had Cunovalos and the Celts, Kunovalos.

There are known to have been three distinct O'Connell septs in Ireland; the O'Connaill's of Derry, in the north; the O'Conaill's of Galway in the west and the O'Conaill's of Kerry which, together with Limerick, Cork and Dublin, are the counties where the majority of the O'Connells, as today the name is usually spelled, are now to be found. Connell—without the prefix—is rarely seen, though up to the middle of the last century it was quite common to drop the O'.

The O'Connells of Kerry were ancient Irish chiefs who changed through the centuries to landed gentry with a strongly European outlook. During the eleventh century the O'Donoghues drove the O'Connells from east to west Kerry. Maurice and Daniel are the two recurring names in the O'Connell saga. Maurice, the head of the Kerry family, was transplanted to a bleak part of County Clare near Lisdoonvarna.

In the seventeenth century many emigrated to France and other parts of Europe where they distinguished themselves in the Irish Brigades and other regiments on the continent.

Maurice (Murty) O'Connell, who was born in Kerry in 1730 entered the Austrian service as a young man of twenty-two and changed his name to Moritz, 'being better suited,' as he said, 'to German orthography'. During the Seven Years War (1756–1763) he was fighting on the Austrian side while his kinsman, Count Daniel O'Connell was on the Prussian side, a not unusual occurrence in those times when so many Irishmen gave their services to the courts of Europe. And, like a number of others of his generation, Moritz O'Connell caught the eye of Maria Theresa, giving him the entrée to the office of imperial chamberlain which he held for fifty-nine years, serving a succession of Austrian emperors. In the army he had reached the seniority of general. He was created a baron and died in Vienna aged over ninety-two.

His cousin and contemporary, Daniel O'Connell (1743–1833), the youngest of twenty-two children, was an officer of Clare's Regiment in France at fourteen, an unusually tender age. He had a distinguished career in the army and was with it right up to the time of the French Revolution. His military talents were outstanding and he was tempted by both Dumouriez and Carnot to take on a high command in the Revolutionary army, which he refused. A monarchist at heart, he joined the hopeless intrigues in favour of its restoration. After the Revolution he returned to Ireland. He tried to interest Pitt in re-organizing the Irish Brigade, but had no success. In 1803 he went to France to see his wife and look after his property when he was imprisoned by Napoleon until the restoration of the Bourbons. Appointed once again a General in the army of France, he lost all his emoluments in 1830 when he refused to take the oath of fidelity to Louis Philippe. He had the unusual distinction of drawing full pay as a General in the French army while acting as a Colonel in the service of the British. He died at Meudon aged ninety.

His nephew was Daniel O'Connell (1775–1847) one of the towering figures of nineteenth-century Ireland. Born at Carhen, County Kerry, he seems to have been neglected by his parents and was looked after mostly by a rakish uncle— Maurice O'Connell (1727–1825), one of the gentry who was also a smuggler and was commonly called 'Hunting Cap'. Like so many of the Catholic Irish gentry who were not permitted an education at home, Daniel O'Connell went to France for his schooling, but had to leave when the Revolution broke out. He studied for the Bar in London and began a very successful law practice in Ireland during those fateful years of 1798–1800. A forceful orator he spoke out strongly against

Daniel O'Connell (1775–1847), 'The Liberator', who achieved Catholic Emancipation for Ireland

the Act of Union, and began to rouse the people to demand the emancipation of Catholics from the penal laws. Balzac said of him that he 'incarnated a whole people'. He became their idol, though he taunted them out of their slavish lethargy. He succeeded in getting himself elected M.P. for Clare in 1828 and when he took his seat in the House of Commons, which hitherto no Irish Catholic had been permitted to do, he had crashed the barriers and forced the grant of emancipation. In 1832 he was elected M.P. for Dublin. The Union was proving very adverse for Ireland, economically and politically, and to reverse it O'Connell founded the Repeal Association in 1840. He began to hold his famous 'monster meetings' in every town and village. Cleverly he combined the

35

passions of religion with nationalism and at one time was sentenced to imprisonment, but the House of Lords had him released.

The new generation—the Young Irelanders—did not revere 'the Liberator' as he was called. At all times he sought to achieve the sovereignty of Ireland by non-violent means. The Young Irelanders insisted on guns rather than strategy. Broken in health and spirit, and foreseeing the terrible famine to come, O'Connell struggled against the inevitable, both in Ireland and in the House of Commons. On a pilgrimage to Rome he died at Genoa in 1847. He was one of the few Irishmen who have changed the entire attitudes of his fellow Irishmen, to have given them the notion that united they could achieve at least some of their ends.

'The Liberator' had had a serene home life—his former home in Merrion Square, Dublin, is still extant—though none of his four sons were of his stature. Maurice (1803–1852) and John (1810–1858), were both politicians and lawyers. But Morgan (1804–1885) followed the other family calling— the army. On a wave of popular feeling at the time, he went to the aid of Simon Bolivar in South America. Subsequently he served for some years in the Austrian army. He tried Irish politics for a while but quarrelled with his father on the subject so close to his heart—repeal of the Act of Union.

Two of the O'Connell family distinguished themselves in Australia. Maurice Charles Philip, a General in the French army, transferred after the Revolution to the British army. He served in the East and West indies and was awarded the governorship of New South Wales and a knighthood in 1834.

Sir Maurice Charles O'Connell (1812–1879), his son, spent ten years in the British army. Returning to Queensland he took a prominent part in Australian politics for which he received his knighthood.

Although the O'Connell name is infrequently mentioned by the leading annalists, it is known that there were bishops and scholars at various times. Peter O'Connell (1775–1826) kept a school in his native County Clare. He tried to win the great Daniel O'Connell's patronage for his Irish-English dictionary, but 'the Liberator' had no feeling for the ancient tongue. The manuscript of his life's work is now housed by the British Museum—it was rescued by another scholar, Eugene O'Curry, after its creator had been forced to pawn it.

Frederick O'Connell (1876–1925) was also a scholar. He had his education from Trinity College, Dublin, and was for a period a parson of the Church of Ireland. In Connemara where he was born, he had become a Gaelic speaker and after the death of his wife he devoted himself completely to linguistics and in particular the Irish language, writing many erudite books. Known by his colleagues as Conall Cearnach he was one of the first directors of Radio Eireann.

Father Daniel O'Connell's family can trace their lineage back to the seventh century. Although he is of the same sept as 'The Liberator', he was not named after him. Daniel is as traditional a name in the family, as Garret is with FitzGerald and Justin with MacCarthy. Daniel O'Connell was born in Rugby, England, in 1896. His parents died when he was young and he came to Ireland to be educated, beginning his clerical studies at seventeen.

He became a scientist of world repute as both astronomer and seismologist. From 1938 until 1953 he was director of the Jesuit observatory at Riverview, New South Wales, Australia. He left there to become director of the Vatican Observatory in Rome. He remained there for eighteen years until his resignation in 1970.

O'CONNOR (O'Conor)

I N the history of Ireland the O'Connors are so numerous, so important and so varied in their activities that an encyclopaedia would not do them justice. *The Dictionary of National Biography* lists nineteen O'Connors and it is believed that few families can trace their descent through so many generations of legitimate ancestors. In the Genealogical Office at Dublin Castle, in France, Spain, Austria, repose many of their pedigrees and papers. The O'Connor people stand out on the pages of Irish history, highlighting the triumphs and the tragedies.

The O'Connors of Connacht are one of the most important branches of this wide-ranging family.

From Conchobhar, King of Connacht, who died in 971, the Connacht O'Connors derive their name. In the Irish form it means a hero or champion and Conchobhar was of a long line of Connacht kings when kings needed to be champions to maintain their supremacy. From Conchobhar descend two High Kings who were monarchs of all Ireland.

Miss Josephine O'Conor of Clonalis House, Castlerea, County Roscommon, holding one of its treasures, an O'Conor pedigree, headed by Milesius, the legendary Spanish king, c.1300 BC, from whom the Irish are supposed to have descended

Conchobhar had to submit to the mighty Brian Boru, King of Munster, who assumed the chief sovereignty and gave Ireland a unity she has not known since. Later, the O'Connors contended with neighbouring chieftains, particularly the powerful O'Rourkes by whom Hugh O'Connor was slain in 1067.

In 1119 Turlough More O'Conor was High King of Ireland. Less of a warrior, more of a statesman, he tried to centralize his government and he built stone bridges and castles and had a fleet of boats on the Shannon and the Atlantic. He maintained a mint to coin silver money. He also plundered from every part of the country, as was the custom. His three marriages gave him twenty children.

One of his sons, Roderic, succeeded to the High kingship. His reign coincided with the invasion from England which led to the Treaty of Windsor in 1175. Kings of England now became lords of Ireland and Roderic held his Kingdom of Connacht only as a vassal of English royalty. Like many of the O'Connor kings, he retired to a monastery to end his days in prayer. He died at Cong, County Galway, in 1198.

Another of Turlough's sons was called Cathal Crobhdhearg (of the red hand). He succeeded his brother Roderic when he abdicated. Cathal Crobhdhearg had close dealings with two kings of England, King John and King Henry III, and letters written by him in Latin are preserved. According to the annalists, he died in 1224, a member of one of the monasteries which he had founded, Ballintubber Abbey, known as 'the abbey which never died'. Mass has been celebrated there without a break since Cathal's time and today Ballintubber has been restored.

From Turlough also descend the three main branches of the O'Connors of Connacht. These are the family of O'Conor Don, O'Conor Roe and O'Conor Sligo. The present O'Conor Don is a Jesuit priest and is the direct descendant of Turlough. His sister, Miss Josephine O'Conor, guards Clonalis House, Castlerea, County Roscommon, a treasure house where manuscripts, documents, books and pictures range over a period of seven hundred years. Clonalis House is the only house open to the public which is wholly of the old Irish, as distinct from those who arrived after the Anglo-Norman invasion.

Of the previous O'Conor home, Belnagare, is left no trace, but in it were born, in widely separated generations, a remarkable group of four O'Conor scholars. The scramble for royal power had long since been replaced by the search for scholarship.

Charles O'Conor (1710–1791), the antiquary, succeeded to Belnagare in 1749. As a Catholic he was debarred from many of the aspirations natural to a country gentleman, but he got a classical education from a Franciscan friar who may also have inspired him to start collecting Irish manuscripts. The blind harpist, Turlough O'Carolan, often stayed in his house. Charles O'Conor corresponded with Dr. Samuel Johnson and other notable contemporaries.

His two grandsons were also scholars. The Reverend Charles, born at Belnagare (1767–1828), was educated at Rome and after a short spell as a pastor in Roscommon, left to become chaplain and librarian to the Duke of Buckingham who had invited him to arrange and translate his collection of manuscripts. At Stowe, the Duke's home, he worked avidly and encouraged by the financial help of the Duke, published his great work *Rerum Hibernicarum Scriptores Veteres* which was printed at the Duke's expense. Tragically, he was stricken by mental illness and he returned to die in County Dublin in 1827. The Duke left many valuable manuscripts relating to Ireland to the Royal Irish Academy in Dublin.

The Reverend Charles O'Conor's brother, Matthew (1773–1844), was also educated for the priesthood in Rome, but changed to the Bar. Using the documents acquired by his family, he wrote *A History of the Irish Catholics* and other specialist works.

Charles Owen O'Conor Don (1838–1905), although several generations later, was also of the scholarly family from Belnagare. He was educated at Downside, near Bath, and was an M.P. for Roscommon until he was defeated by the Parnellites. He also was a writer and he sat on many royal commissions and, in 1881, was President of the Royal Irish Academy. He wrote a history of his family, *The O'Connors of Connacht.*

Arthur O'Connor (1763–1852), M.P., United Irishman, and later General under Napoleon

In spite of their scholarly tendencies, by no means all the O'Connors had quit the battlefields. Arthur (1763–1852), of the numerous Munster O'Connors, was born into a wealthy County Cork family. He studied for the Bar at Trinity College, Dublin, became an M.P. and then he joined the United Irishmen. He was arrested and tried for high treason and was imprisoned several times, eventually in 1803, being deported to France. Here he met Napoleon in whose army he became a general. Arthur O'Connor married Elisa Condorcet, daughter of the French philosopher.

Roger, Arthur's brother (1761–1834), also studied for the Bar at Trinity, and joined the United Irishmen. He, too, was arrested, sent to Fort George, Scotland, and eventually released. But there ends the similarity between the brothers. Roger was more than an eccentric. His Dangan Castle home burned down after a strangely heavy insurance cover. He eloped with a married woman. He was tried for robbing the Galway mail—he had but wanted to obtain from it some letters incriminating a friend, he said. Then he took to writing imaginary annals and crazy books.

There were two notable O'Connor painters. James Arthur O'Connor (1791–1841) was born in Dublin and became an engraver like his father. Finding it not sufficiently creative he changed to landscape painting and he went to London where his pictures were exhibited at the Royal Academy. Although his pictures were recognized as possessing extraordinary merit, he died a poor man. At one stage he was invited to work at Westport House, County Mayo, the seat of the Marquess of Sligo, of the Browne family. Many fine examples of his painting hang there. Today an Arthur O'Connor commands a high price.

John O'Connor (1830–1889), born in County Derry, began as a call boy in a

Dublin theatre from which he rose to become a scene painter, which led to his being transferred to Drury Lane and to London's leading theatres. Here he took to serious painting, exhibited at the Royal Academy and attracted the attention of the nobility. He was noticed by the royal family who commanded him to record many of their ceremonial occasions.

Andrew O'Connor (1874–1941) was a sculptor of international repute. The statue of Abraham Lincoln at his birthplace in Kentucky is his work. Christopher Columbus at Genoa is also by him. A pupil of Rodin, his ecclesiastical sculpture was ahead of its time from the viewpoint of the Irish hierarchy.

There have been many prominent politicians in the O'Connor family. The most remarkable of these was undoubtedly Feargus, son of the eccentric Roger. Born at Connorville, Cork in 1794, he took part in the reform agitation and was elected an M.P. for County Cork. When he was unseated in 1836 he founded a committee of radical unions in England. From these unions sprang the Chartist movement of which he became the virtual leader. He was sentenced to eighteen months' imprisonment for seditious libels. Later he became an M.P. for Nottingham. His behaviour became so outrageous that mental instability had to be acknowledged and he was placed in a home where he died aged fifty-nine.

In succeeding generations the O'Connors continued to distinguish themselves abroad in the military sphere—there was no opportunity for them to practise their profession legitimately at home.

General Luke Smythe O'Connor (1806–1873), born in Dublin, served in both East and West Indies and was governor of Gambia in 1852. Colonel Charles O'Connor of the Irish Brigade was an officer in the Royalist army in France. Sir Luke O'Connor (1832–1915), born in Elphin, County Roscommon, enlisted in the ranks of the Royal Welsh Fusiliers and won a V.C. and a commission for his bravery at the Alma.

General Gerard O'Connor was in the wars of independence in South America early in the last century. Here he raised a regiment at his own expense and joined the Irish Legion under D'Evreux. He fought through all their campaigns in Venezuela and New Granada and he accompanied Bolivar to Peru where he served as his Chief of Staff.

Two brothers of the O'Connor Kerry sept, Michael O'Connor (1810–1872) and James (1823–1890), were both bishops in America.

Some families dropped the O' prefix, as did Patrick Edward Connor (1823–1890) who fought on the Confederate side in the American Civil War.

Charles O'Connor (1804–1884) was born in New York city where he was admitted to the Bar in 1824. After the Civil War he became senior counsel for Jefferson Davis on his indictment for treason.

It would be difficult to group the O'Connors of more recent times, so diverse were their careers. Sir Nicholas Roderick O'Connor (1844–1908) of Roscommon, had a rewarding career in the British diplomatic service where he served in Berlin, Madrid, Washington and Paris before becoming Minister at Peking from 1892–1895. As Ambassador at St. Petersburg he attended the coronation of Czar Nicholas.

Thomas Power O'Connor (1848–1929) of Athlone, graduated from the university at Galway and went to London to work as a reporter. From 1880–1885 he was a Nationalist M.P. for Galway. In 1924 he was 'father' of the House of Commons. Famous in the publishing world as T. P. O'Connor, he founded and edited many newspapers, including *The Star*.

John O'Connor (1850–1928) of Cork had a rudimentary education followed by experience as a van driver and commercial traveller. He was a Fenian leader and an M.P., but sacrificed his seat because he remained faithful to Parnell. Under the Coercion Act he was imprisoned five times. He was called to the English Bar in 1893, and was Prior of the Johnson Club before he died in Hampstead, London, aged seventy-eight.

James Charles O'Connor (1853–1928) of Cork, was educated in Trinity College, Dublin, and in Germany. He became 'the father and pioneer of the Esperanto movement in the English-speaking world'. He translated the Gospel of St. John into Esperanto and wrote many standard works on the subject.

Sir James O'Connor (1872–1930) a lawyer who was born at Wexford, had, according to *The Times*, 'a career which was, we believe, without precedent in England or in Ireland. Starting as a solicitor, he was called to the Irish Bar, became successively a Law Officer, a Judge, and a Lord Justice, and after retirement was re-admitted a solicitor.' He also found time to write a *History of Ireland*.

In 1906 Peter O'Connor of Thurles was the holder of the world record for the long jump. At the Olympic Games in Athens that year he also won a Gold Medal in the Hop, Step and Jump, and when the Union Jack was hoisted at the presentation of the medal he climbed the flagstaff and replaced it with the flag of his native land. This first Irish flag to be hoisted for an Olympic victory was there to proclaim he had won for Ireland, rather than for England.

Frank O'Connor, one of the greatest of modern Irish writers, was not an O'Connor at all. He took the name as a pseudonym and he will be found under his family name of O'Donovan.

Joseph O'Connor was born in Dublin in 1916. An actor-writer, he has written a number of plays of which *The Iron Harp* is best known. He won the Foyle Award in 1955.

Connors, possibly an anglicization of O'Connor, is also the clan name of many of the travelling people of Ireland.

Bronze bust of the writer Frank O'Connor by Seamus Murphy R.H.A.

O'DALY

THE O' is seldom used to prefix this very common name. It derives from an Irish word meaning a place for holding assemblies. Dail, the name of the Irish parliament, is from the same root. It is an apt name for the O'Dalys who were leaders of Irish bardic literature for almost seven hundred years. They are said to be descended directly from one of the epic heroes, Niall of the Nine Hostages, the High King, who ruled at Tara, in Meath, from 380 to 405.

The O'Dalys were originally chiefs of Corca Adhaimh in Westmeath. The scholarly John O'Donovan (1805–1861) writes, 'There is certainly no family to which the bardic literature of Ireland is more deeply indebted than that of O'Daly.' Between 1139 and 1680 no less than thirty distinguished O'Daly poets are recorded.

The first of this poetic family was Cuconnacht na Scoile (Cuconnacht of the School), who died at Clonard in 1139. He was the forerunner of the line of bardic O'Dalys of whom O'Donovan also wrote, 'From this time forward poetry became a profession in the family, and Corca Adhaimh sent forth poetic professors to various parts of Ireland.' Cuconnacht O'Daly set up a bardic school—hence the nickname—in his native Westmeath and from there O'Daly poets fanned out all over the country, settling down as official poets to leading families.

Everywhere they went there was a place for them. In Cavan they became the traditional poets to the O'Reillys, while the branch who went north became poets to the foremost family of Ulster, the O'Neills. In Connacht the O'Connors had an O'Daly poet, and at Finvarra, in the Burren country, they stayed with the O'Loghlins who were lords of Corcomroe. They went to West Cork to the MacCarthys, the ruling family of Munster.

Donogh Mor O'Daly (d.1244), the most famous of these hereditary poets has been fulsomely described as 'the Irish Ovid'. He wrote thirty poems of great length, and mostly religious. He died at Boyle in Roscommon and was buried in the Cistercian Abbey there which was suppressed in 1569. Today its ivy-clad ruins stand close by the River Boyle on the main road.

The poets were not always sweet-tempered. In 1213, Muiredach O'Daly, whose home was by Lough Derravaragh, the Lake of the Oaks, where the legendary children of Lir were turned into swans, left his Westmeath headquarters to visit the O'Donnells at Drumcliffe, near Sligo. One of their stewards treated him badly and Muiredach killed him. For this crime the O'Donnells pursued him all over Ireland until he escaped to Scotland, and from there he wrote a poem to O'Donnell in such appealing terms that he was forgiven and allowed to return home.

Not so another O'Daly who also fell from grace. This was Aengus, the renegade poet from Cork who was employed by the English to record his own countrymen. He wrote a bitter satire, the notorious *Tribes of Ireland*. Foolishly he returned to Ireland in 1617 where a Meagher of Roscrea, who had been denigrated in *The Tribes* took his revenge by stabbing him to death.

Daniel O'Daly (1595–1662) was an outstanding European. Born to a Kerry family who vigorously opposed the Elizabethan conquerors in Ireland he had to be educated on the continent. He entered the Dominican Order of Preachers at Lugo, Galicia, taking the name Dominic de Rosario. He was a Professor at the Irish Dominican College which he founded at Louvain in Belgium and he also founded a college and a convent at Lisbon for Irish religious exiles. His diplomatic skill must have been considerable for he was employed by European monarchs in the most delicate negotiations. The Prince of Wales (Charles I) thought of requesting him to seek the hand of the Infanta Isabella from her father Philip IV of Spain. In Portugal he was prominent in the revolution of 1640 which freed it from Spain and was appointed Confessor to the Queen of Portugal, Luis de Guzman. In 1650 Charles II and his mother, Queen Henrietta-Maria, summoned him to Paris to urge him to use his influence to effect a coalition of the Irish royalists against the Parliamentarians. O'Daly wrote to Ormonde, the Lord-Lieutenant of Ireland, assuring him of his readiness to serve the royal cause in Ireland as well as Spain, but only as soon as an assurance was received from the king that the Irish should be established as a free nation.

In 1656 O'Daly was used as envoy from Portugal to Louis XIV at Paris to advise on military matters concerning the Irish. He died at Lisbon, leaving many important ecclesiastical writings.

Until the early nineteenth century the Daly lineage had, with few exceptions, continued their role as poets. However, with the arrival of Richard Daly (1750–1813), came a change of emphasis. The second son of a County Galway gentleman he was sent to Trinity College, Dublin. He was addicted to gambling and duelling and soon lost his patrimony. This led to his making use of his elegance and striking stature for a career on the stage. In this he was very successful. In 1781, when Dublin was one of the leading cities of Europe, he opened the famous Smock Alley Theatre where Kemble and Mrs. Siddons appeared under his management. By 1786 Richard Daly was a proprietor of the Crow Street Theatre and a patentee of Dublin's Theatre Royal. He had a stormy career in the theatre and won a libel case against one of his fiercest opponents, John Magee, a newspaper critic.

The Dalys who were Barons of Dunsandle, were direct descendants of Donogh Mor O'Daly, 'the Irish Ovid'. They were politicians and men of the law.

Denis Daly (1747–1791) was an M.P. for Galway in 1786. He opposed a measure of independence and received the office of Muster Master General with its salary of £1,200 a year. He also opposed Flood's bill for parliamentary reform. Despite his unpopular views, his friendship with Henry Grattan, the leader of the Irish opposition, remained unbroken. Grattan described his early death as 'an irretrievable loss to Ireland'. He also said: 'Had Daly lived there would probably have been no insurrection. He would have spoken to the people with authority and would have restrained the government.' He had a great reputation as a speaker but was regarded as indolent, though good-humoured and fond of books. Those in his library sold well after his death for they were many and valuable.

Cloghan Castle, near Banagher, is one of the oldest inhabited castles in the Republic of Ireland. It was built in 1120, by John MacCoughlan at the expense of his wife, Sabina O'Daly. In its long and dramatic history it has had many owners. In 1967 it returned via the Dalys of Dunsandle to Major Denis Bowes Daly.

Dennis Daly (1747–1791), M.P. for Galway and renowned speaker

Lack of education was never a handicap however impoverished the Dalys. John O'Daly (1800–1873), born at Farnane, Waterford, got his education in one of the hedge schools which grew up because the Penal Laws prevented Catholics being educated. John O'Daly benefited from his *al fresco* schooling, developing into a scholar and a bookseller. In Dublin he set up a bookshop in Anglesea Street. Irish was his great interest and he issued many valuable works on it and made translations which the poet, James Clarence Mangan, turned into verse. He died esteemed by all the Irish scholars.

The parents of Charles Patrick Daly (1816–1899) had emigrated to New York City. They were very poor and his education was scanty. He went to sea as a cabin boy and spent three years before the mast—he was at Algiers in 1830 when the French captured it. Returning to New York he apprenticed himself to a master carpenter. At night he studied avidly and he joined a literary society. Encouraged by those who saw his talents he was able to enter a law office and was admitted to the Bar, the seven-year term of studentship being varied in his case on account of his brilliance. He practised in New York City and joined the Democratic party, and at the age of twenty-eight was made a judge, remaining a member of the Court for nearly forty-two years, as a Chief Justice. It was said of him that he 'followed the course his instinct convinced him; was dictated by principle, totally regardless of public opinion or party sympathies'. He never forgot his sea-faring days and for more than thirty-five years he was President of the American Geographical Society. He wrote voluminously on historical aspects of law.

John Augustus Daly (1838–1899), who was born in Plymouth, North Carolina, was the son of Captain Denis Daly, a ship owner whose family had come from Ireland. John Augustus Daly was to be the founder of one of New York's best known theatres, Daly's Fifth Avenue Theatre, where Ada Rehan (1860–1916), the Limerick-born actress, was the leading lady for many years. It was this Daly who introduced melodrama to the theatre, anticipating the cinema. He held his audiences entranced, waiting for the rescue of seemingly helpless victims bound to the railroad tracks in the path of the onrushing train. He was also a superb producer of Shakespeare.

It seems fitting that an Irish-American should be the first to promote the plays of George Bernard Shaw in America. This was Arnold Daly (1875–1927), the Brooklyn-born son of Irish parents. In 1903 he put on a single matinee production of *Candida* at the Prince's Theatre, New York, with Dorothy Donnelly as leading lady and himself as Marchbanks. It went down so well he rented the Berkeley Lyceum where *Candida* ran for one-hundred-and-fifty performances. It was the start of the Shaw vogue in America and he put on other Shaw plays until he ran up against Mrs. Grundy. He violated the law with *Mrs. Warren's Profession* and was arrested with his leading lady, Mary Shaw. He was tried in Special Sessions, but acquitted. He revived several Shaw successes although he was mainly interested in a theatre of ideas. He refused to advertize in newspapers or to give free seats to critics. He ran into serious financial difficulties, a victim, it was suggested, of his own temperamental excesses.

Marcus Daly (1841–1900) was born in Ireland and went to America with his parents, Luke and Mary Daly. They were exceedingly poor and at fifteen Marcus Daly was working as a pick-and-shovel man. He displayed such ability he attracted the attention of some mining experts who sent him to Butte, Montana, where he rapidly grew very knowledgeable. In partnership he bought the Alice Silver Mine and, with George Hearst, the Anaconda Silver Mine, and when the silver gave out he closed it and quietly bought up all the other mines and caught the great copper boom. Butte and the Anaconda mines were famous and in twenty years Marcus Daly amassed a huge fortune. A man of wide interests, he developed fruit growing in Montana and he owned and trained some of the finest and fastest horses. His good fortune never went to his head and he kept in touch with his former pick-and-shovel friends and gave them considerable help.

Chicago is regarded as one of the best run cities in the United States of America. It has to be admitted that much of the credit for this goes to Mayor Richard Daley who has dominated its civic institutions for several decades. He was born there in 1902, the only child of Michael Daley who had emigrated from Waterford. He was a sheet metal worker and his wife was Lillian Dunne of Limerick parents.

In Ireland the Daly name comes into prominence again in the legal profession. In 1946, Cearbhall Ó Dálaigh, the Irish form of Carol Daly, was Ireland's youngest Attorney General at the age of thirty-five. In 1972, Chief Justice Ó Dálaigh was appointed Judge of the Court of Justice of the European Communities which sits at Luxembourg. For Ireland the E.E.C. is a renewal of strong personal and diplomatic links which existed with the Continent long ago.

DILLON

DILLON is another prime example of a Norman name which has become Irish, and is most distinguished both at home and in Europe. It came to Ireland with the Norman invasion, with Sir Henry de Leon of Brittany whose name was Hibernicized to Dillon. Large grants of land in Westmeath were bestowed on Sir Henry by the Earl of Moreton, later King John of France and England. The Dillons populated it so thoroughly it became known as 'Dillon's Country', and Sir John's heirs were barons of Kilkenny West, while another branch of the Dillons settled in County Mayo. The present Lord Dillon is the 19th Viscount Dillon of Costello-Gallen in the county of Sligo.

The first Viscount Dillon, Sir Theobald, was a direct descendant of Sir Henry and it seemed logical he should continue to support his royal benefactors in the reign of Elizabeth I. In 1559 he is reported to have commanded an independent troop in the royal cause, for which he received a knighthood on the field of battle. Shortly before his death in 1624, James I created him Viscount Dillon of Costello-Gallen. Theobald himself died at so advanced an age 'that at one time he had the satisfaction of seeing above an hundred of his descendants in his house of Killenfaghny'.

Sir James Dillon of Proudstown, another kinsman of the original Sir Henry of Brittany, 'was ancestor of the Dillons, Earls of Roscommon, of the Dillons, Lords of Clonbrock, and of the Dillons, Baronets and Barons of the Holy Roman Empire 1782, and of the Dillons of Proudstown and Skrine, Barons of the Holy Roman Empire 1767, now extinct', according to *Burke's Peerage and Baronetage* which devotes four pages to the Dillons.

Wentworth Dillon, 4th Earl of Roscommon, son of James the 3rd Earl of Roscommon and Elizabeth Wentworth sister of the Earl of Strafford, was born in 1633 and had a wide-ranging education abroad. After the Restoration he lived somewhat raffishly in England, visiting Ireland only briefly.

He married Lady Frances, daughter of the Earl of Burlington and devoted the latter part of his life to literature. He is credited with being the first major critic to recognize the genius of Milton's *Paradise Lost*. Pope called this Earl of Roscommon, 'the only moral writer of King Charles' reign. . . . He improved taste if not enlarged knowledge.' In 1684 he died and was buried in Westminster Abbey. The Roscommon title remains dormant.

Thomas, the 4th Viscount Dillon, of the Westmeath branch, was born in 1615 and was reared a Catholic. At fifteen he adopted the new religion and subsequently was able to take his seat in Parliament. They were hazardous times and on a mission for King Charles about 1641 he, and another Irish nobleman, Lord Taaffe, were arrested at Ware in Hertfordshire by order of the House of Commons. Some months later Thomas managed to escape to join King Charles at York. On his return to Ireland he was made Lieutenant General and, with Viscount Wilmot, he was appointed Joint Lord President of Connacht.

In 1646 he was received back into the Catholic Church at Kilkenny by the Papal Nuncio, Rinuccini. Thomas Dillon then fought for the Irish, commanding a division of Ormond's army, but they were defeated outside

Dublin by the Roundheads under General Michael Jones. After this disappointment Ormond handed over the Sword of State and temporarily quitted Ireland.

Upon Cromwell's arrival in 1649, Thomas Dillon's estates were confiscated and he fled with his family to France until the Restoration. By 1665 most of his extensive lands were restored but he died, some years afterwards, aged fifty-eight. His family appear to have had a house in Winetavern Street, Dublin. His wife and one of his sons are buried in the nearby churchyard of St. James.

Another kinsman, Sir James Dillon, was a M.P. for County Westmeath from 1639–1642. After the Cromwellian wars he, too, went with his entire family to France where, in 1653, he raised the famous Regiment of Dillon. He became a Field Marshal and died in France in 1668.

Count Arthur Dillon was born in 1670. It is said his mother was one of the civilians killed by a shell fired into the besieged city of Limerick. After it was taken, eleven thousand soldiers of Ireland's last great army sailed for France with most of their officers. Meanwhile, the young Count Arthur Dillon was already in France and was to become a Colonel in Dillon's Regiment. The history of this regiment can be more fully explored in O'Callaghan's *History of the Irish Brigade*, and in books written about the Irish in France by Richard Hayes.

Count Arthur Dillon served for forty years with the French army, becoming a Field Marshal and, later, a Governor of Toulon. He has been described as tall and handsome, a good officer and a brave soldier. He died in 1733, aged sixty-three, at St. Germain-en-Laye, but his *Memoirs* perished, alas, during the Revolution. He had four daughters, and five sons, four of whom served in the French army, while the fifth, Arthur, became Archbishop of Toulouse and Narbonne—a rather unexpected appointment.

This is how the appointment came about. Colonel James Dillon, one of the numerous Dillon sons in France, commanded the Irish Brigade which drove back the English column at Fontenoy after it had penetrated the French lines. James fell in battle and King Louis XVI, who had seen him in action, the following day ordered his brother, Arthur, then a modest curé, to be given the next vacant benefice. Arthur Dillon rapidly rose to become Archbishop of Toulouse and Narbonne, and President of Languedoc. From this, the largest province in France, he had an annual income of £40,000 from church property. His way of life was far from austere. He had a salon in Paris and was a constant courtier. His stables were envied by Louis XVI who once asked why he hunted while his clerics were forbidden the sport. 'My vices are the vices of my ancestors, my priests' vices are their own,' was his acid reply.

Nemesis eventually caught him. In 1788 his expenditure so far exceeded his income he went bankrupt. When the French Revolution came with its anti-religious laws, an inflexible royalist, he refused to take the oath which meant he had to flee France. He died an exile in London in 1806.

Nor had things gone as he would have wished in his immediate family. The nephew he had reared, Count Arthur Dillon, later became a revolutionary and a general of the Republic. This nephew had even tried to capture his uncle when he heard the Archbishop of Toulouse and Narbonne was hiding in Verdun!

Of five brothers, sons of a Dublin banker who had emigrated to Bordeaux, two were priests, Henry and Arthur. Another was Count Edward, 'le beau Dillon', a favourite of Marie Antoinette's. In fact he was accused of being one of her lovers, which seems to have been an invention of her jealous courtiers. When the Bastille fell he was en route to France from Egypt. He was gentleman-in-waiting to the Duke of Artois, the King's brother. Later, from Coblentz, he tried with his brothers to reform the Dillon Regiment to help in the invasion of France. When all seemed lost for French royalism, Count Edward went to Ireland, with

The brave but unfortunate
COUNT DILLON,
A General in the French Service
who fell a Victim to the mistaken rage of his own Soldiers
on the 29th April. 1792.

those Irish officers who had fled from France, where, ironically, he recruited an Irish Brigade for service in the English army.

Had conditions allowed the Dillons to use their talents in Ireland as they had so generously for France, what a different story there might have been in the eighteenth century. In his memoirs Louis Philippe, Comte de Ségur, mentions that when en route to Russia as envoy for Louis XV at the Court of Catherine II, he 'was accompanied by Count O'Kelly and Monsieur Dillon'. Which of the many Dillons does not seem necessary for him to elaborate. The Dillons in France were very many. In Bordeaux they were among the leading citizens and their adherence to Arthur, Edward, Theobald and James as names for their sons could be confusing.

A Dr. Edward Dillon was Superior of the Irish College at Douai. It was closed as a result of the Revolution and he returned to Galway, to become Bishop of Tuam. He preached so firmly against the United Irishmen, and the principles of the French Revolution, that he was disliked and distrusted both by the Unionists and the patriots.

Theobald, Count Dillon, born in Dublin in 1745, followed his kinsmen to France to become a Field-Marshal, having gained experience with Washington in the American War of Independence. He was a Colonel of Dillon's Regiment which, at the outbreak of the Revolution, was stationed at Lille. All foreign legions in the army were abolished then and Dillon's Regiment was incorporated in one of the regular troops. Theobald became a General of the Cavalry Brigade. The Regiment of Dillon had by that time been commanded for one hundred and one years by successive members of the same family. Following the revolution it became merely the 87th Regiment.

Several other Dillons also went over to the revolutionary side. For Theobald Dillon there was a tragic denouement. In the war against Austria in 1792 he was ordered to make a feigned attack at Tournai. This was misunderstood by the cavalry who, turning on its own infantry with cries of 'We have been betrayed,' massacred all mercilessly. Theobald's hip was shattered by a bullet and later, still thinking 'The aristocrat Dillon' had betrayed them, his own troops murdered him and burned his body. Amends were made afterwards for this madness and he was accorded the honour of burial in the Pantheon.

The daughter of a Colonel Arthur Dillon who had been guillotined, married Count Bertrand and, together, they became distinguished for their fidelity to Napoleon. They were with him when he died on St. Helena.

In the Dillon family there have been scholars as well as men of the sword. John Talbot Dillon of Lismullen, County Meath (1740–1805), was M.P. for Wicklow in 1771, and was created a Baron of the Holy Roman Empire in Vienna by Emperor Joseph II in recognition of his services to Catholic interests in parliament. He travelled widely and was a recognized expert on Spain. He was a linguist and a very objective observer. His principal work is his *Historical and Critical Memoirs of the General Revolution in France, 1789–1790*. These memoirs gave a contemporary view of the seeds of the Revolution and included many contemporary documents.

Captain Peter Dillon (1785–1874) joined the French Navy. In his voyaging he acquired a considerable knowledge of the South Sea Islands and had the Legion of Honour conferred on him by Charles X of France, plus an annual pension of 4,000 francs. In 1829 he published an account of his travels.

John Blake Dillon (1816–1866), member of the Young Ireland Party

John Blake Dillon was born in County Mayo in 1816. For a brief time he studied for the priesthood, then changed to Trinity College, Dublin, to study for the Bar. There he met Thomas Davis and other young men who were forming the Young Ireland party in opposition to Daniel O'Connell's abhorrence of violence. With Gavan Duffy he helped in the founding of their paper, *The Nation*, and after the failure of their abortive rising in 1848, John Blake Dillon had to hide on the Aran Islands until his escape to France. From there he went to America where, with other exiles, he practised at the New York Courts. Following the amnesty of 1855, he returned to Ireland and to politics. In 1865 he was M.P. for Tipperary, but he died from cholera the following year.

His son, also called John Blake Dillon, succeeded him in the Tipperary seat. It was the time of the rising sun of Charles Stewart Parnell and the Land League, and John Blake Dillon, no less than the others, had his share of imprisonment.

A grandson of his, James Dillon of Roscommon, has twice held the post of Minister for Agriculture in the Government of the Republic of Ireland.

James Dillon's brother, Professor Myles Dillon (1900–1972) was a scholar of wide repute. He held a number of posts abroad, in America and England and he lectured on an international scale. He was a Professor at the School of Celtic Studies and was a Director of the Celtic School in Dublin's Institute for Advanced Studies. He edited many learned publications on early Irish literature.

Gerard Dillon, a native of Belfast, for over thirty years held his place as one of Ireland's leading painters. A retrospective exhibition of his pictures was held, first in Belfast, then in Dublin, shortly after his death in 1972.

The Dillon name is very widespread, particularly in Meath and in the West of Ireland. The various off-shoots of the family have had many seats at home, as well as in France. Probably the best known of the Dillon strongholds is Portlick Castle, north of Athlone, a fourteenth- to seventeenth-century fortress by the shores of Lough Rea.

O'DONNELL

NIALL of the Nine Hostages who was High King from 380 to 405, was raiding Britain and Gaul when the Romans were withdrawing. One of his many sons, Conall, settled in Ulster, in Tir Conaill—Connell's territory, today known as Donegal. From him descend the O'Donnells of Tyrconnell, for many centuries one of the most powerful Irish families. There were also O'Donnells in West Clare and further south in Limerick and Tipperary.

At Kilmacrenan, north of Letterkenny, their chiefs were inaugurated on Carraig Dun. Here, in 1248, Godfrey O'Donnell (d.1258) was made 'O'Donnell', chief of his clan. In common with the O'Donnells of medieval times he occupied himself in tribal warfare, mostly with his own kinsmen, the O'Neills.

The O'Donnells of Tyrconnell played a leading role in striving to preserve their territories from subjection to the English crown. When it seemed to their advantage they joined with the English against the O'Neills. Sometimes they found it more opportune to be allied with the O'Neills against the English.

They had close links with Scotland. Calvagh O'Donnell (d.1566) went there for help in wresting the lordship of Tyrconnell from his father.

A most poignant episode in Irish history was the kidnapping of fifteen year old Red Hugh O'Donnell (1572–1602). He was enticed aboard a merchant ship on Lough Swilly which immediately sailed for Dublin. There he was imprisoned in the Castle for three years. At Christmas Eve, 1591, Red Hugh and two young O'Neills escaped, suffering great hardships on a three day trek across the snowy Wicklow mountains. Art O'Neill died, but Red Hugh, helped by both the O'Byrnes and O'Tooles of Wicklow, reached Tyrconnell where his father relinquished the chieftainship to him. Red Hugh vigorously harried the English and devastated much of Connacht. In 1601, learning of the arrival of the Spanish at Kinsale, he marched south, only to be involved in that disastrous defeat. Red Hugh went to Spain where he died mysteriously, it is suspected by poison administered by a spy.

Rory (1575–1608), Red Hugh's brother, succeeded him, but joined the flight of the Earls to Spain in 1607. It was from that time that the O'Donnells began to feature prominently in the armies of Europe.

A descendant of the Earls of Tyrconnell, Leopold O'Donnell, Duke of Tetuan (1809–1867), a statesman and a general in the army of Queen Christina of Spain, was Governor of Cuba from 1844 to 1848.

James Louis O'Donnell (1738–1811) of Tipperary was one of the many O'Donnell church dignatories. His missionary zeal took him to Canada where he was appointed bishop and was known as 'the Apostle of Newfoundland'.

Patrick O'Donnell (1856–1927) from Letterkenny was a bishop at thirty-eight —the youngest bishop in the Catholic hierarchy. A constitutional nationalist, he strove to make peace and goodwill take the place of the religious bigotry peculiar to the province of Ulster. He became archbishop of Armagh in 1924 and in 1925 was created a cardinal.

In the United States of America, Thomas Jefferson O'Donnell (1856–1925),

Two princes of the O'Donnells: Sir George (1832–1889) and Sir Richard (b.1834)

son of Irish emigrants and a relative of Daniel O'Connell, became one of the most noted trial lawyers of the Rocky Mountain region of Colorado.

In Ireland the O'Donnells were prominent in politics and literature. Peadar O'Donnell born in 1893 in Donegal, a strong nationalist, was deeply involved in the problems of small farmers and labourers. He abandoned teaching for trade union organization and fought in the civil war in Ireland. Later he joined the various left-wing movements in Europe. In the thirties he produced a play and a stream of novels. One of Ireland's finest literary magazines, *The Bell*, now defunct, had its final years under his editorship.

A jewelled casket containing a Latin psalter said to have been written by St. Columba, known as the 'cathach of Colum-Cille', was a battle talisman carried by the O'Donnells. The psalter can be seen at the Royal Irish Academy in Dublin while the casket is in the National Museum. 'The Four O'Donnell Pearls', supposed to have belonged to Red Hugh O'Donnell, are now in private possession in London.

O'DONOGHUE (Donohoe, Dunphy)

B ECAUSE of the anglicization of Irish names there are a number of different versions of this very numerous name, a name particularly common now in south west Cork and Tipperary. It is formed from a personal name, Donagh, 'brown warrior'. There are several distinct families as well as variations of the spelling. It was anglicized to Dunphy by the Ossory branch, who were of the same stock as the Fitzpatricks, who founded the Cistercian Abbey of Jerpoint in Kilkenny. This was built by the king of Ossory, Donagh MacGillapatrick, in 1158, about the period when surnames were beginning to be formed from first names. In 1387 the abbot of Jerpoint was fined for a violation of the Statute of Kilkenny which prohibited the admission of Irishmen as members of the community. The abbey was suppressed in 1540 and its lands were given to the Butlers, the great family of Ormonde. It is one of the finest of the many monastic ruins in Ireland.

The O'Donoghues of Cashel, Tipperary, though related to the all-powerful MacCarthys, were frequently in territorial conflict with them which led to the eventual submergence of this O'Donoghue sept which had descended from Donagh, son of Ceallachan, king of Cashel.

The O'Donoghues of Desmond were kinsmen of the O'Mahonys, descendants of the kings of Munster. They were among the many prominent families present at the battle of Clontarf in 1014.

By the fourteenth century the O'Donoghues had been driven out of their territories by the MacCarthys and the O'Mahonys. They settled in Kerry where they became lords of all the country around Killarney. Here they separated into two distinct clans. Their chieftains were O'Donoghue Mor and O'Donoghue of the Glen. Ross Castle by the Lakes of Killarney, today a graceful ruin, was the headquarters of the O'Donoghue Mor family.

In far-off times an O'Donoghue of the Glen was supposed to have gone over to the fairies. According to the legend, on May Day he used to glide over the Lakes of Killarney on a white horse accompanied by the sound of unearthly music and attended by troops of spirits scattering flowers. It would be nice to think that it was this unearthly manifestation which helped the O'Donoghues of the Glen to retain their considerable property until recently. That rare and special Irish title O'Donoghue of the Glen is still extant.

Their kinsmen, the O'Donoghues of Ross Castle, had their lands confiscated in the reign of Elizabeth. They became the property of the now extinct family of the Earls of Kenmare.

After the Battle of the Boyne in 1690 the O'Donoghues began to be mentioned in European and South American history. An O'Donoghue exile in Spain became O'Donoju, while Juan O'Donoju (1751–1821) was the last Spanish ruler of Mexico. O'Donoghue features in the military lists of France, Spain, Austria.

Those who survived at home were active in politics. Daniel, The O'Donoghue (1833–1889), born in Kerry and educated at Stonyhurst, was M.P. for Tipperary. Afterwards he became a prominent figure in national politics—Charles Gavan Duffy regarded him as an extreme nationalist. He was challenged to a duel by

Sir Robert Peel who had called O'Donoghue a 'Mannikin traitor'. In 1870 he went bankrupt.

Patrick O'Donoghue, another patriot O'Donoghue of that time, was tried at the Clonmel Assizes with O'Brien, Meagher and MacManus and was sentenced to death which was tempered to transportation for life to Van Dieman's Land.

Daniel O'Donogue (1833–1889), M.P. for Tipperary and for Tralee, an extreme nationalist

There were also O'Donoghues in the arts. Francis Joseph (1875–1911) was Dublin born. He studied painting in Paris and exhibited at the Royal Hibernian Academy in 1899. He was one of the early victims of the motor car—he was killed in an accident in Morehampton Road, Dublin, in 1911.

John O'Donoghue, a lawyer and a Kerry Journalist, became editor of *The Freeman's Journal* in 1871. He wrote *The Historical Memoirs of the O'Briens*. He died in 1893.

David James O'Donoghue (1886–1917), born in London of Cork parentage, returned to Dublin to set himself up as a bookseller. He edited *Poets of Ireland*, a most useful reference book.

John O'Donoghue tried life from various angles; policeman, monk, labourer in England and, finally, writer. His many times rejected reminiscences, *In a Quiet Land*, brought him fame and was a Book Society choice. He was working on his fourth book in 1964 when he died.

O'DONOVAN

I N his book, *Irish Names and Surnames*, Father Woulfe says that the O'Donovans belong to the royal race of Munster and that they were originally chiefs of Carbery, a district lying along the river Maigue in County Limerick. Their principal stronghold was at Bruree, in Irish 'Brugh Riogh', the Royal Residence. Donovan, in Irish, is a combination of donn (brown) and dubhan (a derivative of dubh, black). With the arrival of the Normans they were driven from Carbery around 1178, and were forced to take refuge in south west Cork where, with the aid of their old allies the O'Mahonys, they settled.

Until the close of the Jacobite wars they held considerable power and extensive possessions. Some O'Donovans moved to Kilkenny, while another branch settled in Waterford and the name is still very numerous in the south of Ireland.

The officially recognized Chief of the name O'Donovan lives now at Skibbereen, West Cork. His sept is described in *Burke's Landed Gentry* as one of the most ancient families in Ireland, with a pedigree traceable back to Callaghan, King of Munster in 964. Callaghan's son was Donovan who ruled as Chief in 977, and it was from him that they took their name. Seventh in descent from him was Crom O'Donovan who possessed Crom Castle by the river Maigue in County Limerick. He had three sons from whom descend all the families of the O'Donovans. The Chief of the name in 1560 was inaugurated by the great Mac-Carthy Reagh.

In the time of James II the O'Donovans favoured the Catholic cause. Because of this allegiance they lost all their power and possessions and many of them went to France where they joined the continental armies in the service of the Irish Brigade. O'Donovan's Infantry was one of the foremost of these many regiments of Irish exiles.

In 1843 Rhoderick O'Donovan, Lieutenant Colonel of the 87th French Infantry, the old Regiment of Dillon and O'Mullaly, was permitted legally to reside in Ireland (he was the first of his family to return after one hundred and fifty years of exile). He married Marguerite Josephine Ida Lally-Tollendal of France, a descendant of an illustrious Irish family whose name had once been Lally of Tullaghnadaly in the County of Galway. Count Lally Tollendal was of this family, a nobleman of both Ireland and France.

During the French Revolution when the Irish nobility in France were also suffering from the excesses of the Jacobins, there was an Abbé Donovan, a Capuchin friar from Cork, who was chaplain to a noble Parisian family. There is a story that the family fled from Paris, leaving the Abbé Donovan in charge of their house and its treasures. He was, however, arrested and condemned to death. In the tumbrils on the way to execution with the other victims to whom he continued to give spiritual comfort, an officer of the troops guarding the guillotine called out in Irish, 'Are there any Irish among you?' 'There are seven of us,' answered the Abbé Donovan. At once the officer used his influence and saved the lives of his fellow countrymen. Father Donovan returned safely to Cork to devote himself, it is said, to preparing condemned prisoners to meet their death.

John O'Donovan (1805–1861)

John O'Donovan (1805–1861), the fourth son of Edmund O'Donovan and Eleanor Hoberlin of Attateemore, was born on a Kilkenny farm. These O'Donovans were proud of their lineage and could trace it back to Eoghan, King of Munster about AD 250, and on his deathbed John's father reminded him of his ancestry. The eldest son took John to Dublin and educated him there. He came under the influence of his uncle, Patrick O'Donovan, who instilled in him a great love for Anglo-Irish history and traditions. He worked first in the Irish Record Office, then in the Ordnance Survey, examining ancient manuscripts in the Irish language where he checked no less than 144,000 ancient place names and his research was so thorough that he corrected the mistakes of many eminent historians of previous ages. In 1845, after working on it for twelve years, he published his *Irish Grammar*. His finest achievement was the translation, annotation and editing of the first complete edition of *The Annals of the Four Masters*. It had been compiled in the reign of Charles I by Michael O'Clery and other monks of the Franciscan Order and is an invaluable history of Ireland from earliest times until the seventeenth century. In recognition of his scholarly editing of this masterpiece John O'Donovan was awarded an honorary LLD by Trinity College, Dublin.

Eugene O'Curry (1796–1862) the Gaelic scholar, said of it, 'The translation is executed with extreme care—an immense mass of notes contain a vast amount of information, historical, topographical and genealogical . . . There is no instance of a work so vast being undertaken and completed in a style so beautiful by the enterprise of a private publisher.' The Irish type for the Annals was cast from designs by George Petrie and it was printed in Dublin by Michael H. Gill.

His literary gifts—of a very different order—were passed on to his son, Edmund O'Donovan (1844–1883), who studied science and medicine at Trinity College but did not graduate. He worked for a while as Clerk to the Registrar, and as Assistant Librarian. He developed such a taste for heraldry he was chosen by Sir Bernard Burke, Ulster King of Arms, to carry a banner at the installation of the Duke of Connaught as Knight of Saint Patrick.

In 1866 he began contributing to the *Irish Times* and other Dublin newspapers. Then he went to France and America and in 1870, during the Franco-German war, his adventurous temperament led him to join the French army. After Sedan he changed to the Foreign Legion which provided him with many adventures about which he wrote accounts for several Dublin papers. During the Carlist rising in 1873 he was in Spain, whence he sent back reports which were published in *The Times* and *The Hour*. In 1876 he was in Bosnia and Herzegovina during the battle against the Turks. He became war correspondent for the *Daily News* and went to Asia Minor to report the war between Russia and Turkey.

Representing the *Daily News*, he made a celebrated journey to Merv and penetrated undisguised in the midst of the Turks who thought him an emissary of the Russians and kept him in captivity. He was a very good linguist and managed to talk himself out of jail and when he reached home, wrote an account of it in his book, *The Merv Oasis*. He was attached to the army of Hicks Pasha which was annihilated at Obeid in 1883. Nothing was ever heard again of Edmund O'Donovan, though it was eight years before probate was allowed, for it was felt he might yet extricate himself from this adventure as he had from so many others. He was one of the first and most daring of war correspondents.

A famous O'Donovan in Irish political history was O'Donovan Rossa. He was born Jeremiah O'Donovan (1831–1915) at Roscarbery, County Cork, and he worked for a while as a relieving officer at Skibbereen but soon became deeply involved in the Fenian movement. He was tried for complicity in a subversive plot known as 'The Phoenix Conspiracy', though eventually released. During 1863–1865, he was business manager of *The Irish People*, the newspaper of the Young Irelanders. With O'Leary, Kickham and other Fenians, he was sentenced to penal servitude for life by the notorious Judge Keogh. In prison in England he was remarkably badly treated but wrote so effectively about it he was amnestied. He was given no option but to go and live in America from where he edited the *United Irishmen* and wrote books about his prison life and recollections. He died, aged eighty-four, in New York and his body was brought back to Dublin where there was one of the largest funeral ceremonies ever witnessed in Glasnevin cemetery. It was shortly before the 1916 revolution and Patrick Pearse, one of its most active instigators, gave a rousing oration at the graveside.

Gerald O'Donovan born in 1871, a Catholic priest who left the church to become a successful businessman in London was, as well, a remarkably talented novelist. He gives an original account of Ireland at the turn of the last century as seen by a priest. Only since her death, has he been revealed as the lifelong friend, probably lover, of the novelist, Rose Macauley.

The vein of literature in the O'Donovans runs strongly. Michael O'Donovan was the world-famous writer Frank O'Connor. He was born in Cork in 1903 and educated by the Christian Brothers and there began work as a librarian. When he died in 1966 he had been compared to Chekhov and de Maupassant, had become the foremost writer of modern Irish literature. In his early years he had been greatly influenced by Daniel Corkery, nationalist writer and Professor of English at University College, Cork. O'Connor's first story, *Guests of the Nation*, published in 1931, is a classic. It tells of the conflict between England and Ireland as seen from the viewpoint of a group of men who would have been friends, rather than killers of each other, had it not been for their history and politics. His short stories are among the most moving and most graphic of modern times and have set a high standard for today's Irish writers. A scholarly writer, his strength was rooted in the Gaelic language and culture and he was often trenchantly critical of progress which involved the destruction of the human environment. He made poetic translations of classics like Brian Merriman's *Midnight Court*. He wrote plays for Dublin's Abbey Theatre and lectured abroad on literature.

DOYLE

G ENEALOGISTS now seem to agree that the origin of Doyle might be Norse, a theory which is supported by the prevalence of Doyles along the coastline of Leinster and Munster. It is thought to be derived from the Irish word for foreigner, dubh-ghall, i.e. dark stranger. In Irish it is O'Dubhghaill and it is mentioned in the *Annals of the Four Masters*. Along the seacoast of Counties Wicklow, Wexford and Carlow the Doyles are very numerous.

Doyle does not appear in the genealogies of the prominent Gaelic families and it is only in the eighteenth century that it begins to be recorded.

Sir John Doyle (1756–1834), soldier, M.P. and Governor of Guernsey

Sir John Doyle (1756–1834) was educated at Trinity College, Dublin, and in 1775 he sailed for America with the 40th Regiment. He spent most of his active service in the British army overseas, first in America, then in France and in Holland. He served under the Duke of York as a Lieutenant Colonel. He was, for a while, a M.P. and Secretary of War in Ireland. On an expedition to Egypt under Abercrombie in 1801, although he was ill in bed, he got up and rode forty miles through the desert to defend Alexandria against the remnants of Napoleon's army. He was created a baronet in 1805 and later became a General. He was Governor of Guernsey.

Sir Charles William Doyle (1775–1843) served with distinction in the 14th

James Warren Doyle (1786–1834), forward-thinking Bishop of Kildare and Leighlin

Foot and was on active service for thirty-seven years on all the battle fronts of Europe, the Near East and the West Indies. He attained the rank of Lieutenant General and was Commander-in-Chief of the army of reserve.

James Warren Doyle (1786–1834), born in New Ross, became the famous Bishop of Kildare and Leighlin, known as 'JKL', i.e. John Kildare and Leighlin. An Augustinian monk, he had a cosmopolitan education. His studies at Coimbra University were cut short by the arrival of Napoleon and, for a while, he acted as an interpreter with Wellington's army. Home eventually in Ireland he became Professor of Rhetoric at Carlow College.

At first his rough appearance gave him little authority with his students. It was not long before they understood they had a teacher of deep knowledge and original thought. He even dared hope for a union between the Established and Catholic churches. He wrote vehemently, under his 'JKL' initials, on the state of Ireland and he three times gave evidence before a London Parliamentary committee who found him most impressive. 'You have been examining Dr. Doyle,' a person remarked to the Duke of Wellington. 'No, but he has been examining us,' said the Duke. Dr. Doyle restored church discipline and built schools and the cathedral in Carlow in which he was buried at the age of forty-eight. A statue by Hogan commemorates him there.

John Doyle (1797–1868), who signed himself 'HB', created brilliant caricatures, chiefly of political persons. A man of strong beliefs, he threw up a lucrative job with *Punch* in repugnance at their vicious cartooning of the Pope. It has been said of him that 'The charm of "HB" was the excellence of the humour shown in the portraits, added to the fact that he did not, as too many political satirists have been prone to do, degenerate into coarseness and vulgarity.'

His son, Richard Doyle (1824–1883), inherited his father's gift and designed the famous title page of *Punch*. He illustrated many books and painted fanciful pictures of witches and elves.

Richard Doyle's son was Sir Arthur Conan Doyle (1859–1930), the Edinburgh-born novelist and creator of the great detective, Sherlock Holmes.

There were also some very well-known Doyles who were not in fact Doyles at all, though few would recognize them by their real name. One of these was 'Martin Doyle' whose real name was William Hickey (1788–1875). A County Cork Protestant clergyman, he tried by his writings to encourage the peasantry to improve their farming methods. With the help of Thomas Boyce he established an agricultural school at Bannow and set up the South Wexford Agricultural Society, the first of its kind. He wrote numerous books on practical topics, especially on landlordism and horticulture.

In the first half of this century Lynn C. Doyle was a household name in Ireland. It was the pen name of a bank manager from Downpatrick, Alexander Montgomery (1873–1961), who wrote some of the most popular and humorous plays and stories. He was the first Irish writer to be appointed to the Censorship Board, from which he resigned in 1937.

The book illustrator Richard Doyle (1824–1883), father of Sir Arthur Conan Doyle

O'DUFFY
(Duhig, Doohey, Dowey, O'Dubthaigh)

THE Irish form of O'Duffy, O'Dubthaigh, means black, referring more likely to the raven locks of the O'Duffys rather than to their swarthiness. The name is quite common all over Ireland, though in the south it has been sometimes varied to Duhig. In the north, where English and Irish are given a different pronunciation, it could be transformed into Doohey or, maybe, Dowey.

In Connacht, near Strokestown, where one branch of the O'Duffys had their patrimony, the town of Lissyduffy still remains as evidence of their former lordship.

The O'Duffys were outstanding churchmen, particularly in Ireland's golden age when her scholars and monks had close ties with Europe. In 1175 it is recorded that King Roderick O'Conor sent an O'Duffy, Archbishop of Tuam, as his ambassador to Henry II of England.

One of the treasures of Dublin's Museum, the Cross of Cong, was made by an O'Duffy in 1123 to the order of Turlough O'Conor, King of Connacht. The O'Duffys embellished many of the churches and monastic settlements which were so vital a part of Irish life.

The number of O'Duffy parish priests recorded in the diocese of Monaghan is quite remarkable. The most famous of these, Owen O'Duffy, lived in the sixteenth century and was an outstanding preacher. He is remembered for his forthright denouncement of the notorious Miler Magrath, the ambivalent Bishop of Cashel and also of Down, who changed his religious allegiance as often as it was profitable and was also twice married.

Edward Duffy (1840–1868), the Fenian leader, was born at Ballaghaderreen, Co. Roscommon, in 1840. He was arrested in Dublin and jailed, but because of ill health he was liberated. He promptly went back to Fenianism and was again arrested and sentenced to fifteen years. He died in London, in Millbank Prison, aged twenty-eight.

In the last century, James Duffy, born in Monaghan, founded the Dublin printing firm of James Duffy and Company which still exists.

James Duffy was a silversmith and jeweller in Dublin and his son, Patrick Vincent, born there in 1832, became a painter of note. A member of the Royal Hibernian Academy, he was a regular exhibitor until his death in 1909.

The Monaghan family of Duffy made rich contributions to the political and educational life of Ireland and Australia. The parents of Charles Gavan Duffy (1816–1903) were not wealthy. His father died young but his mother educated him well—he added her name, Gavan, to his father's. He went to Dublin to become a journalist, a co-founder of *The Nation* and a member of the Young Ireland party. After the party's downfall and his own trial for sedition he entered Parliament. He was delicate, and Ireland offered no opportunity for a man of his calibre. He went to Australia and rose to be Prime Minister of Victoria in 1871. He was knighted in 1873 and retired to the South of France in 1880, where he wrote profusely about Irish History and about Australia. He died in Nice in 1903. He married three times and had many children.

His eldest son, John Gavan Duffy (1844–1917), though born in Dublin, also became a member of the Victoria government. The next son, Frank, was Chief Justice of the High Court of Australia and was knighted—as was Frank's son, another Charles Gavan Duffy, who was a Judge of the Supreme Court of Victoria. The third son was Clerk of the Houses of Parliament of Victoria and the fourth son, Philip, was a pioneer in railway engineering in Western Australia. A daughter by his second marriage, Louise, returned to Ireland where she was a pioneer of the Irish language, though she had an English mother. She founded and was headmistress in a remarkable school for girls—remarkable in that it was secular and it taught all subjects through the Irish language. Scoil Bhride still flourishes in Dublin.

Charles Gavan Duffy (1816–1903) who went to Australia where he became Prime Minister of Victoria

Eimar O'Duffy (1893–1945), the son of a Dublin dentist, was also a dentist himself though he never practised. Instead, after an experimental period in Irish politics—he did not favour the rising of 1916—he retreated to England where he immersed himself in literature. He wrote novels and satirical essays of which *King Goshawk and the Birds* is probably the best known.

The life of General Eoin O'Duffy (1892–1944) is a strange tale in modern Irish history. Born in Castleblaney, Monaghan, he was a military leader with Michael Collins. He was imprisoned in Belfast. During 1921–1922, when the Irish Free State was formed, he was General Officer Commanding its forces. He was also Chief Commissioner of the Civic Guards. When removed from these appointments after Eamon De Valera came to power, he joined the opposition and began his campaign against communism, forming the Blue Shirt organization, based on similar fascist groups of the thirties. In an effort to restore his once great prestige he recruited 1,400 volunteers to join Franco's 'holy crusade against Bolshevism' in Spain in 1936. After a taste of battle they lost heart and returned home ignominiously after six months. It was the end of O'Duffy's once promising career.

To many Irish children Duffy means but one thing—Duffy's Circus. For three generations they have been travelling Ireland with their clowns, bareback riders and performing animals. The ringmaster and head of the family, Mr. James Duffy, died in 1973. His six brothers are all directors of the circus.

FITZGERALD

S INCE their arrival with the Norman invasion of 1170 the Fitzgeralds have played a major role in every crisis in Ireland. Any account of Irish history omitting the Fitzgeralds would be impossible. At one period a member of this family—the great Garret Mor—was recognized by both the Irish and the English as the uncrowned king of Ireland. Rather than remaining aloof like the English, they consciously integrated by culture and marriage with the Irish and their reward was commensurate.

Maurice, son of Gerald, Constable of Pembroke, was one of the companions of Strongbow on his invasion of Ireland, and from him the very numerous families of Fitzgerald are descended. Maurice received large grants of land which were in the possession of his descendants until quite recently. Fitzgerald means son of Gerald—Fitz (French fils) becoming Mac in Irish, hence MacGearailt. The head of the Leinster branch was Earl of Kildare, later, Duke of Leinster, while the head of the Munster Fitzgeralds was the Earl of Desmond. Between 1329 and 1601 there have been sixteen Earls of Desmond. Twenty Earls of Kildare are recorded between 1326 and 1766, then the title changed to Duke of Leinster, of whom there have been eight.

The Fitzgeralds are well recorded. An account of any one of them, at the minimum, fills a chapter of history. It is only possible to select a representative few as the pageant flicks past.

In 1176 the manor at Maynooth, County Kildare, was granted by Strongbow to Maurice Fitzgerald who built a castle for protection against the natives. Three centuries later his descendant, Garret Mor, the Great Earl of Kildare, founded a college close to the castle. This college was suppressed by Henry VIII, but in

Maynooth College today

1795 the English government founded St. Patrick's College there as a seminary for Roman Catholic clergy who, because of the Revolution, could no longer be educated in France. By this gesture it was hoped to win their loyalty. Today Maynooth, a constituent college of the National University, is open to all students, including women.

It was a John, Earl of Desmond who, by virtue of his powers as a Count Palatine, created his three sons hereditary knights; Knight of Glin, Knight of Kerry and the White Knight. The first two are represented today but the White Knights are extinct. The Knight of Kerry is today the 23rd, and Desmond John Villiers is the 29th Knight of Glin, Keeper at the Department of Furniture and Woodwork at the Victoria and Albert Museum and an adviser on Irish Decorative Arts to the Ulster Museum. Glin Castle near Limerick remains his family home.

Gerald Fitzgerald, Garret Mor, the Great Earl (d. 1513), was all but king of Ireland and was the only ruler since Brian Boru who came anywhere near to giving it unity. Through the reigns of three English sovereigns he was Lord Deputy. He knew how to hold power and he believed in those marriage alliances on which family power rested. Although Irish women wield much power from the hearth, in law they are not so well regarded. Garret Mor used his five daughters to consolidate his territories, marrying them off to Burke of Clanricard, Sir Piers Butler (later Earl of Ormond and a bitter enemy), Lord Slane, and, flouting the Statutes of Kilkenny which forbade marriage with the native Catholic Irish, to the chiefs Mac Carthy Reagh of Muskerry and O'Carroll of Ely.

In an unsuccessful attempt to oust the Tudors, Garret Mor supported Lambert Simnel who was crowned Edward VI of England and Ireland in Dublin in 1487. From this *faux pas* Garret Mor, however, managed to extricate himself.

He introduced artillery to Ireland, and used it to quell his enemies. For forty years he ruled, 'a mighty man of stature, full of honour and courage, open and plain, hardly able to rule himself when he was moved to anger, easily displeased and soon appeased, of the English well beloved, a good justiciar, a suppressor of rebels and a warrior incomparable'. Under him there was a new sense of nationality, and the influence of the Renaissance was beginning to be felt. His castle at Maynooth was richly furnished with fine things, including books and manuscripts.

However, he finally displeased Henry VII and from 1494 to 1496, languished in the Tower of London. Accused by the Archbishop of Cashel of burning down his cathedral he answered, 'I would not have done it if I had not been told that my Lord Archbishop was inside.' This delighted the king and when someone exclaimed, 'All Ireland cannot govern this Earl,' Henry VII rejoined, 'Then let this Earl govern all Ireland.' He returned to Ireland, once more as Lord Deputy.

Gerald Fitzgerald, 9th Earl of Kildare, was said to have been one of the handsomest men of his time. Hans Holbein painted his portrait. After a chequered career he died in the Tower of London in 1534.

His daughter, the Lady Elizabeth Fitzgerald, was 'The fair Geraldine' immortalized by Walter Scott and other poets. She was a first cousin of Henry VIII and had been brought up with the Princesses Mary and Elizabeth. She was twice married, firstly at a very early age to a man of sixty-one. She is buried beside her second husband, the Earl of Lincoln, in St. George's Chapel, Windsor Castle.

The Lady Elizabeth's brother, known as Silken Thomas because of his colourful attire and that of his retinue, renounced his allegiance to Henry VIII, allying himself with the Irish lords, many of them his own cousins. Eventually he was captured and became the third generation of the Fitzgeralds to be imprisoned in the Tower of London. In 1537, at the age of twenty-four, together with his five uncles, he was executed at Tyburn. On the walls of the prison may still be seen the letters 'THOMAS FITZG. . . .'—the name was never completed.

He was succeeded by his brother, Gerald, aged eleven, who spent years in hiding with the O'Conors, O'Briens, MacCarthys, all blood relations. The Tudors were determined to exterminate the Fitzgeralds, so Gerald, the heir, was smuggled abroad. 'For the people conceite more to see a Geraldyn to reigne and triumphe, than to see God come amongst theym.' Gerald was educated in France with the Dauphin, and in Rome where, in 1545, he was appointed master of horse to Cosmo de Medici. In Queen Elizabeth's reign, conforming to the Protestant religion, he was received into favour in 1552 and had his estates restored to him. But treachery was afoot and he followed the beaten path, the fourth generation of the Geraldines to be imprisoned in the Tower of London. He died there in 1585.

Around the Countess of Desmond (a Fitzgerald title), second wife of the 12th Earl of Kildare, the legends proliferate, mainly concerned with her physical durability. In her old age she was very poor and had to walk many miles to market and it is said she carried her sixty-year-old daughter on her back when she herself was ninety. In 1589 she was visited by Sir Walter Raleigh. It has now been confirmed she died aged one hundred in 1604, not one hundred and thirty-four, and possibly not from falling out of a cherry tree, as the legend tells she did. In Muckross House, Killarney, which is open during the summer, there is a portrait of her in her great age.

It was Robert, the 19th Earl of Kildare, who, in 1744, purchased Carton, having decided his castle of Maynooth was too dilapidated. Carton was designed by the famous Richard Castle who built a number of houses for the Irish gentry between 1728 and 1751, the year he suddenly died there. A picture of the Earl and one of his wife, Lady Mary O'Brien, hangs at Carton, County Kildare, which is open to the public from May to September.

Before moving to Carton, the 19th Earl had been living at Kilkea Castle, County Kildare. Now an hotel, it is said to be haunted by the 11th Earl, the Wizard Earl who sleeps in the Rath of Mullaghmast, from which he emerges from time to time to ride round the Curragh on a white horse shod with silver shoes.

Carton is one of the Fitzgerald houses which displays their famous coat of arms incorporating the monkey. Several legends have gathered around the appearance of this little animal in the Kildare family bearings. One is that when John Fitz Thomas, afterwards 1st Earl of Kildare, was an infant in the castle of Woodstock, it caught fire and, in the rush for safety, he was forgotten. However, a pet monkey broke its chain, grabbed the infant and carried him to safety in a tower. The Kildares have never forgotten this kindness to humans and have commemorated it even in the plasterwork at Carton. But Jonathan Swift, who quarrelled with the then Earl of Kildare, filched the Kildare monkey, using it in *Gulliver's Travels*—Gulliver being carried off and fed by the Brobdingnagian ape!

James, the 20th Earl of Kildare, became the 1st Duke of Leinster. Born in

1772 he laid the foundations of Leinster House, Dublin, saying, when told that it was in an unfashionable part of the town, 'They will follow me wherever I go.' Today Leinster House, in Kildare Street, is the Dail, the Irish parliament. James was married to Emily Lennox, daughter of the 2nd Duke of Richmond. She was the guiding light behind the splendid embellishments of Carton. A celebrated beauty, her portrait was painted by Reynolds. Lady Louisa, her sister, married Speaker Thomas Connolly. The Connollys built Castletown, that most splendid Kildare house which is today the headquarters of the Irish Georgian Society, a centre for musical evenings, céilithe, balls and exhibitions.

James and Emily had twenty-two children. The twelfth child was Lord Edward Fitzgerald, born in 1764, of whom his mother wrote in babyhood, 'Eddie carries a sword, the prettiest thing you ever saw, and is reading Marlboro's campaigns.' 'Eddie', who was educated in France, fought on the English side in the American War of Independence. In later years he expressed regret he had fought on the wrong side. He was in Paris during the Revolution and was very impressed by its egalitarian principles. There, also, he met Pamela, the adopted daughter of Madame de Genlis. He married Pamela and brought her home to Frascati by the sea at Blackrock, County Dublin, an intimate retreat bought by his mother, the Duchess of Leinster, from Hely Hutchinson, Provost of Trinity College, Dublin. Their idyll at Frascati was short-lived.

Lord Edward, who had great personal magnetism—during a sojourn in Canada he had been made honorary chief of the Bear Tribe—went into politics and became M.P. for Athy. Seeing no hope of constitutional changes, he joined the United Irishmen and assumed their military leadership. He had to go underground. Eventually in 1798 he was betrayed and died of wounds, aged thirty-four.

Lord Edward Fitzgerald, leader of the United Irishmen (1764–1798)

George Robert Fitzgerald (1748–1786) was no credit whatever to his illustrious family. His father was Robert Fitzgerald of Turlough near Castlebar, Mayo, and his mother was Lady Mary Hervey, sister of the Earl of Bristol. He was brought up in the best of English society and travelled abroad. However, by the time he returned to Ireland in 1775 to become a landlord, his wife, a sister to Thomas Connolly, had left him. His cheating at games, his duelling and

66

his violent behaviour thoroughly discredited him. George quarrelled with his family and locked up his father whom, for a while, he had tied to his pet bear. He kept a private army and was the terror of County Mayo. Eventually, he was condemned to death for killing a man. The rope snapped, but in the two hours before the gallows was finally ready he had ample time to relent and to die penitently.

The Fitzgeralds have had continued representation on the continent. In 1411, the 5th Earl of Desmond who married an Irish peasant girl, was so unpopular he had to abandon his property and begin a new life in Rouen. In the eighteenth century the Fitzgeralds were prominent in the Irish Brigade and the Regiment of Fitzgerald fought valiantly in the War of the Spanish Succession.

Percy Hetherington Fitzgerald (1834–1925) was born in County Louth and studied Law at Trinity College, Dublin. A man of unusual talents, he was not only a prolific writer, he was also a sculptor. In London, the statue of Dr. Johnson in the Strand is his work as is the statue of Dickens at Bath and Boswell at Lichfield.

As scientists, surgeons, lawyers, politicians, writers and colonial statesmen the Fitzgeralds have distinguished themselves. The Fitzgeralds in the New World are almost as numerous as in Ireland. The writer of *The Great Gatsby* and *This Side of Paradise*, Francis Scott Fitzgerald (1896–1940), was an American author of Irish lineage.

In the twentieth century a FitzGerald played a prominent role in the achievement of Irish independence. Desmond FitzGerald, whose parents were from Kerry, was born and educated in London and came to Kerry to study Irish. He was a fine linguist and spoke six European languages. For thirty years, before and after the Treaty, which he supported, he took a leading part in Irish politics. He was a volunteer in the 1916 rising and was sentenced to life imprisonment but was released at the general amnesty. He had the distinction of being elected to three different parliaments: the first Dail, an illegal body, the first Dail under the Treaty, and the British House of Commons. Under the policy of abstention then in force he did not take his seat at Westminster. Because of the misrepresentation of Dail Eireann by the British press he instituted a Department of Publicity. He was a writer, a poet and an Abbey Theatre dramatist. His interest in Thomastic philosophy led to an intimate friendship with Jacques Maritain. For several years he delivered a series of lectures on philosophy at Notre Dame University in the United States of America.

While Minister for External Affairs, Desmond Fitzgerald was head of a department set up to provide a case for the removal of the border. During his tenure the Irish Free State, as it was then, secured recognition by the League of Nations. In 1947 he died, aged fifty-eight.

Garret FitzGerald, one of the four sons of Desmond FitzGerald, was born in Dublin in 1926, graduated from University College, Dublin, and was called to the Irish Bar. He is a T.D. of the Fine Gael party. The most prominent of Irish political economists he writes about economics on which he is regarded as an expert. His book, *Towards a New Ireland*, was published in 1972. He is a former chairman of the Irish Council of the European Movement, and is an energetic speaker and lecturer and Minister for Foreign Affairs.

Today, the name Fitzgerald, sometimes spelt FitzGerald, is very widespread in Ireland and the name Garret is still frequently associated with it.

O'FLAHERTY

T HE O'Flahertys are of the very old Irish. Their armorial bearings spell out their story. The red hand from their dealings with the Ulster O'Neills. The black galley which signifies their ships and the lizard which alerted the sleeping O'Flaherty warrior to the approaching enemy.

There have been many ways of spelling O'Flaherty in both Irish and English. The word itself means the bright ruler. In County Donegal, where the Irish is different, the name became O'Laverty. The O'Flaherty clan to this day is most numerous around Galway, though happily now they are no longer 'The ferocious O'Flahertys from whom God defend us'—an exhortation the citizens of Galway felt obliged to fix to their city gate in the middle ages.

The history of the O'Flahertys, undoubtedly, was one of constant warfare and some very dark deeds. For decades they fought against the native O'Connors and the Norman Burkes, who took over Connacht and by the best possible means, through intermarriage, turned native. The Burkes could not feel secure in their territory while the O'Flahertys were menacing neighbours. They attacked them so fiercely the O'Flahertys capitulated, made a treaty with them and then, aided by the Burkes, turned round and attacked their former allies, the O'Connors! It was all very confusing and wasteful.

Morogh O'Flaherty and his brother, Roderick, when they were once more attacked by the Burkes, took their complaint to Henry III, but they found they had to do their own fighting and did, eventually, quell the Burkes. This made them undisputed masters of a quarter of a million acres of Connacht, from Lough Corrib to the Atlantic, which kept them quiet for several centuries.

For defence purposes they were mostly on good terms with the O'Malley clan of County Mayo. However, they fought and slew an O'Malley and his son, Connor, plundered the O'Malleys' rich castles and sailed away with all their riches. However, he did not get far as he, his men and their ships foundered off the Aran Islands.

The O'Flahertys' magnificent castle, Aughnanure, outside Galway, which stands to this day, was for centuries their fortress. Here they entertained the young Burke who had come to collect a long overdue rent. They sat him down to dine and when he mentioned rent, the stone floor under his chair opened and pitched him into the river beneath. Retrieving his body they sent the head back to the Burkes with a message: 'This is O'Flaherty's rent.'

Queen Elizabeth I whom they called Caileach Granda, the ugly hag, was constantly getting in their way as she tried to subdue them. When the sons of the Earl of Clanrickard (a Burke), rebelled against her and tried to get O'Flaherty aid to fortify themselves, Morogh O'Flaherty betrayed their plans. For this he was rewarded with the patrimony of Donal Crone, the rightful O'Flaherty chief.

Not even Grace O'Malley, 'Gran Uaile', the greatest sea-faring woman of all time, could quell the fighting O'Flahertys.

The Morogh O'Flaherty who had betrayed the Clanrickards (Burkes), was eventually so plundered by the ruffianly soldiers who came with Elizabeth's detested governor, Bingham, that he and his twelve sons surrendered their castles,

Aughnanure Castle, County Galway, for centuries a fortress of the O'Flahertys

titles, Irish customs, but not the O'Flaherty succession. So disillusioned was 'Sir' Morogh—he had been graced with an English title by the 'old hag'—he joined with the O'Neills and O'Donnells of the north to fight at the battle of Kinsale. His descendants were still on the losing side in 1641 and again at the Battle of the Boyne in 1690, so that by the seventeenth century the O'Flahertys who had once lorded over vast tracts of Connacht were landless. It was the end of the 'ferocious O'Flahertys'.

The last of the O'Flaherty chieftains, Roderick, who, aged twenty when Oliver Cromwell took all from his family, appealed to Charles II who gave him back a little of his inheritance. He was a scholar and the little cottage where he settled near Spiddal outside Galway can still be found. In Latin he wrote a famous history of his native province, the *Ogygia*. He wrote until he died in 1709, aged eighty. All his other manuscripts are lost and many of his descendants went abroad, some to Austria.

The Reverend Colman E. O'Flaherty, born in Carraroe, Connemara, in 1874, was ordained in South Dakota in 1901. He worked in the United States for eighteen years, at Columbus College and Notre Dame Academy and he built many churches. He went to France as Chaplain to the 28th Infantry of the American Expeditionary Force and was killed there in 1918.

The most remarkable reincarnation of the O'Flahertys of former days was the Right Reverend Monsignor Hugh O'Flaherty who was born in Kerry, ordained in Rome and earned the name of 'The Scarlet Pimpernel of the Vatican' for organizing escape routes for thousands of allied soldiers out of German-occupied

Italy during the 1939–45 war. After a lifetime abroad he returned to die in Kerry in 1963.

It was a proud day for the O'Flahertys when Michael O'Flaherty of Carraroe was appointed Mayor of Galway in 1949. For centuries the O'Flahertys had been forbidden to hold any office in that city. His son, Patrick, was Mayor of Galway City in 1964.

Stephen O'Flaherty, born in Passage East, County Waterford, in 1905, was one of the first of the Irish millionaire industrialists. Son of an Aran Islander, he was the first to assemble the Volkswagen car outside Germany when he introduced it to Ireland after the 1939–1945 war.

Liam O'Flaherty (b.1897), the writer

Liam O'Flaherty was born on the Aran Islands in 1897, in a community speaking only Irish. A priest sponsored his education but he discovered he had no vocation for the church. He served in the British army during the war, then took a part in the Revolution and Civil War in Ireland. He went to London and began to write. In 1925 *The Informer* established him as an important writer. By many he is rated one of the foremost short story writers. He has lived in California and in Dublin.

O'GRADY

E ARLY in the fourteenth century, for reasons hard to define, a number of the O'Gradys changed their name to Brady, which means that some of the Bradys now plentiful on the north-east side of Ireland may not be Bradys at all. To add to the confusion there were families who changed back to their original Grady name as was done by the ancestors of the present Chief of the Name, who belongs to one of the most ancient families in County Limerick and one of the few whose claim to chieftainship is officially recognized.

He is Lieutenant Colonel Gerald Vigors De Courcy O'Grady who lives at the family seat, Killballyowen, Bruff, County Limerick. It is close to Lough Gur, a small lake around which there is a rich assemblage of ancient monuments, including stone circles, forts, dolmens and other megalithic tombs. Excavations have shown that it was occupied from the Neolithic Period till late Medieval times. Colonel The O'Grady is very knowledgeable about the wild birds which make their seasonal homes on this lake surrounded by low hills.

The O'Grady name—it means noble or illustrious—goes back to a Dalcassian sept who had their territories at Killanasooglah near the river Fergus in County Clare. Around 1318 they moved to Tuamgraney where the O'Briens, their kinsmen, granted them a very generous amount of land in both Clare and Galway counties.

From 1364 to 1371 the Archbishop of Tuam, a very prestigious dignity, was a John O'Grady.

In 1543, Donogh O'Grady was knighted by Henry VIII and was granted by him letters patent to secure the lands of his clan. From then on the O'Gradys adhered to the English side.

Because of the alteration of the name, Sir Donogh's son, who became the first Protestant Bishop of Meath, was confusingly known as Hugh Brady. Thus began the ancestry of the Bradys of Raheen in County Clare.

Another of Sir Donogh's sons who settled in County Limerick and reverted to the O'Grady name, was the ancestor of the present O'Grady of Killballyowen.

Branches of the family lived in several areas of County Limerick. The O'Gradys who lived on the Glenstal estate—it was known as the Cappercullen estate in those days—had a tree on the avenue which became known as the 'Ilchester Oak'. It was under its shade that a beautiful Miss O'Grady was supposed to tryst her lover, Lord Stavordale, son of the Earl of Ilchester. They had met at a ball in Limerick but, because of his own comparative poverty, the girl's father was too proud to approve of their courtship. However, Lord Ilchester did not disapprove and gave his blessing and Mr. O'Grady could do nothing else but follow suit. Today, Glenstal Abbey, a Benedictine establishment, is a boys' school.

Standish O'Grady (1766–1840) was born at Mount Prospect, County Limerick. He studied Law at Trinity College, Dublin, and rose to the office of Attorney General. He was the prosecutor at the trial of the patriot Robert Emmet who subsequently died on the scaffold because of his part in the insurrections of 1798 and 1803. The execution of Emmet had an effect on Irish political sentiment as profound as that of the execution of his counterparts in the 1916 rising.

In 1831, Standish O'Grady, who for many years had been Lord Chief Baron of the Exchequer in Ireland, was created Viscount Guillamore of Cahir, and Baron O'Grady of Rockbarton, both of County Limerick.

His nephew, Standish Hayes O'Grady, became a considerable Irish scholar. Born at Castle Connell, County Limerick, in 1832, he was educated at Rugby School and at Trinity College, Dublin, where he divided his studies between civil engineering and the copying of ancient Irish manuscripts under the expert guidance of John O'Donovan and Eugene O'Curry. However, he abandoned these studies and went to America where he practised engineering for many years. Eventually he left America for London to return to his literary studies. He compiled a catalogue of the Irish manuscripts in the British Museum. At his

Standish Hayes O'Grady (1832–1915), civil engineer and Irish scholar

death in 1915 it was still unfinished, but it was completed by Robin Flower. The *Silva Gadelica* tales from ancient Irish manuscripts, was his principal work.

The third Standish O'Grady (1846–1928) of Castletown Bere in County Cork was also a writer, but of a very different calibre. Graduating to the Bar from Trinity College, Dublin, he turned to journalism and then history. He wrote many historical novels with a romantic Irish setting. His aim was to arouse interest in the Irish past by retelling the ancient, half-forgotten legends of the heroic age. He believed firmly in the existence of Cuculain, Finn, Maeve and all the Celtic heroes.

'How could primitive singers have invented such heroes?' he would argue. The titles of his books were evocative: *The Chieftain's Last Rally*, *Red Hugh's Captivity*, *The Flight of the Eagle*, *The Coming of Cuculain*. He influenced the generation growing up at the turn of the century. Compared to the realism and scholarship of today's historians he is no longer highly regarded.

It is understandable that with so many Standish O'Gradys there is confusion. When Standish, the scholar-engineer, died in 1915 there was much gossip in the English papers which mixed him up with Standish O'Grady, the then living romantic novelist who has also been accused of 'cooking Irish history'.

In the previous century a number of O'Gradys were outstanding in the field of medicine, particularly as surgeons.

In the O'Grady family which is now frequently to be found in Munster and Connacht, there have been numbers of writers and poets, perhaps of most consequence today is the poet and journalist Desmond O'Grady, who was born in Limerick in 1935 and lives now mostly in Rome.

Henry Woodfin O'Grady's ancestry was Irish. Born in 1850 near Atlanta, Georgia, his father, a Colonel in the Highland Guards, was killed during the American Civil War.

Henry O'Grady studied law at the University of Virginia. When he was prevented from exposing the corruption in local politics in the newspaper for which he was working, he bought the other two newspapers and founded a third. When he used his newspapers in an attempt to purge politics the reaction from the citizens was to cease reading his newspapers.

Finding that truth in news reporting did not pay—it also lost him his inheritance—Henry O'Grady went to New York where his sound news sense was appreciated by the *New York Herald*. It was said of him that he had 'a faculty for writing in accord with popular taste'. His far-seeing articles did much to alleviate the misery that came after the Civil War. Speaking on the very thorny negro question he achieved great popularity as a forthright orator. In 1889 he delivered a powerful speech on the American race problem. He died a few days later of pneumonia at the early age of thirty-nine.

Australia can also lay claim to yet another O'Grady writer. Frank O'Grady (1909), born in Sydney, New South Wales, and a Vice President of the Royal Australian Historical Society, has published a number of novels including *The Golden Valley*, *Hanging Rock*, *The Sun Breaks Through*.

Generations of schoolgirls and boys who had their physical training in the classroom were instructed in ringing tones, 'O'Grady says knees bend! O'Grady says feet apart! O'Grady says march to the left!' And so on. It can only be supposed that the original O'Grady was one of the numerous O'Gradys who served abroad with the British army.

MacGUINNESS (Magennis, MacGinis)

LIKE so many Irish names which have been anglicized, there are a number of spellings of this ancient name which originated with the son of Angus who lived in St. Patrick's time. Early records of Irish life are comparatively scant, yet there seems little doubt that from the twelfth century the Magennises were the principal territorial lords of Iveagh in County Down. Art Magennis, the Lord of Iveagh, is mentioned in public records at a very early period and in varied spellings of the name.

The Magennises were essentially a County Down family. Their principal castle and stronghold was at Rathfriland, ten miles from Newry near the Mountains of Mourne. In the uprising of 1641 it was destroyed. Another of their castles, Dundrum, built in the twelfth century on the site of a legendary prehistoric fort, is still to be seen, four miles from Newcastle, County Down. In 1588, to replace an older one, Felix Magennis had built himself a new castle. The only trace of it remaining today is the name of the town—Newcastle.

The inevitable struggle for local power between the Magennises and their neighbours turned to defence with the arrival of the Normans, followed by the less flexible Britons, and the Bruce invasion from Scotland in 1315.

In an attempt to hold on to their castle at Dundrum the Magennises fought continually against King John, against Henry VIII, and his Lord Deputy, Garret Og, Earl of Kildare. Finally, in 1601, it was taken for the English by Lord Mountjoy.

In Tudor times the Magennises would seem to have prudently trimmed their sails for it is recorded that they had remained 'loyal to Queen Elizabeth'. Sir Henry Bagenal, writing in 1582, mentions, 'Magennis liveth very civilly and English-like in his house, and every festival day weareth English garments amongst his own followers.' No doubt that, but a Magennis was uncivil enough to be on the winning side at the Battle of the Yellow Ford in 1598, one of the rare occasions when the Gaels, led by Hugh O'Neill, routed the English.

In 1601, despite the Spanish aid, and the Scottish mercenaries, the battle of Kinsale was a major disaster. From then onwards came the decline of the Gaelic aristocracy who began their flight to Europe, hoping to return another day to fight again in their own country.

Despite the tragic reverse at Kinsale of what had promised to be a triumph, it turned out that the Magennises were among the lucky few who had their County Down lands granted back to them—twenty-two thousand acres in all— and Magennis of Iveagh was created a Viscount by James I. However, Cromwell and his army soon ensured that the old Ulster landowners were deprived of their properties and honours.

In a later generation the savage behaviour of Sir Conn Magennis makes shameful reading. In the mid-sixteenth century he ransacked Newry and cruelly ill-treated or barbarously murdered its Protestant inhabitants. His wickedness appears to have been matched by the Viscountess of Iveagh who is reported to have been equally cruel to the English and Scottish inhabitants of Newry.

74

The Magennis name appears in exalted places in the church. Arthur Magennis was made Bishop of Dromore by Pope Paul III, but changed his allegiance to Henry VIII, while retaining his bishopric in the reformed church. Hugo Magennis, a Franciscan, remained Bishop of Down until his death in 1640.

The Magennises were leaders in the desperate rising of 1641 when they fought side by side with O'Neill, Maguire and MacMahon. The strife was continued and in the following generations was laid the foundation of some of the bitterness which afflicts Ulster to the present day.

In 1689, while the siege of Derry was taking place, James II summoned to

The oldest Irish harp in existence, on which the Guinness brewery has based its trademark since 1876

Dublin an assembly of the Irish Estates called 'The Patriot Parliament'. It was attended by a few Protestant bishops and loyalists and fifty Irish peers. Among the viscounts was a Magennis of Iveagh. It was the last legislative assembly of the older Irish race until 1922 and the last at which the Roman Catholic faith was represented. A year after this assembly came the Battle of the Boyne, a side issue of the European wars pursued by Louis XIV. After the Boyne the Gaelic peers such as Iveagh, Mountcashel, Clare, Clancarthy, vanished from Ireland to reappear again in various European countries.

The 2nd Viscount Iveagh, Brian Magennis, a colonel in Iveagh's Regiment in the Austrian Army, was killed in action in 1703. His brother, Roger, the 3rd Viscount, also fought in France and Spain.

John R. MacGuinness, born in Dublin in 1840, became a General in the army of the United States of America.

Charles Donagh Magennis, born in Derry city in 1867, studied architecture in Dublin, also went to America where he built schools, churches and colleges across the American continent, including the bronze doors of St. Patrick's Cathedral in New York City. In 1937–1938 he was President of the Institute of Architects. He died in Boston in 1955.

Peter Magennis, a farmer's son, was born in Fermanagh. He was a National School teacher and he wrote poetry and novels. *The Ribbon Conspiracy* is his best known work. It dealt with his childhood experiences of the clash between the Orange Lodges and the peasant trade unions. He died in 1910.

The Iveagh title comes back again, revived by a cognate family originating in the County Down. These are the Guinesses whose name has become synonymous with the largest brewery in the world, known affectionately to the Irish as 'Uncle Arthur'.

Arthur Guinness (1725–1803) was the founder of the firm. His grandson, Sir Benjamin Lee Guinness (1798–1868), was Lord Mayor of Dublin, which city he represented in the British parliament. He was created a baronet in 1867. He was famous for his philanthropy and he restored St. Patrick's Cathedral in Dublin when it was almost in ruins. The present chairman of the Guinness company, Lord Iveagh, is a descendant of the founder.

Desmond Guinness and his wife Mariga, at Castletown House, County Dublin, head-quarters of the Irish Georgian Society

Another member of the family, the Honourable Desmond Guinness and his wife, Mariga, have contributed greatly to stimulate the appreciation and restoration of the remaining historic houses of Ireland by their leadership of the revived Irish Georgian Society, both in Ireland and in America.

Today, MacGuinness is far more commonly used than the older form, Magennis, or Guinness. It is to be found all over Ireland, predominating in the north east.

HEALY (Hely)

HEALY is a very common Gaelic name. Only in the Irish, Ó hÉilidhe, is the O to be found today. The Healys or Helys—they are two distinct septs—are said to be descendants of a chieftain of this name, which means scientific or ingenious, translated from the Irish.

The Ó hÉilidhe land was below the Curlew Mountains around the west shore of Lough Arrow in County Sligo. Their seat was Ballyhely—one of several Ballyhelys—and they were gentry until dispossessed by the Cromwellians. The other sept, the Helys of Donoughmore in the barony of Muskerry, County Cork, also suffered similar disturbances.

A number of the Healys were outstanding in the church. Patrick O'Healy, a Franciscan who was educated in Rome and Spain, was the last Bishop of Mayo before it was joined to the see of Tuam in County Galway. The penal legislation caused him to be persecuted and he was tortured and executed at Kilmallock, County Limerick, in 1579.

Father Healy (1824–1894), a parish priest of Little Bray in County Wicklow, was a renowned wit.

John Healy (1841–1918), Archbishop of Tuam, a Senator of the Royal and National Universities, wrote many scholarly works, including a history of Maynooth College.

John Hely-Hutchinson (1724–1794), son of Francis Hely of Gortmore, County Cork, was a lawyer and a provost of Trinity College, Dublin. In 1751 he married an heiress and assumed her family name of Hutchinson. In 1783 his wife was raised to the peerage as Baroness Donoughmore of Knocklofty, County Tipperary. Donoughmore in County Cork was their original home. In his earlier days John Hely is described as 'an obstreperous patriot' and in later days, as a man of 'unblushing venality'.

Unqualified for the exalted position of provost of Trinity College, Dublin, he intrigued his way into being elected. He proved a very efficient provost although he outraged university sentiment and had constant disputes with the Fellows and the students and misused his powers for the advancement of his family. Trinity owes its Modern Languages professorships to John Hely-Hutchinson. Remarkable for his time and position, he supported Free Trade and Catholic reforms.

John Hely-Hutchinson had six sons who distinguished themselves mostly in the cause of England. One son, Richard (1756–1825), the 1st Earl of Donoughmore, also championed the cause of Catholic reform in the House of Lords and he strenuously opposed every attempt to rule Ireland by purely coercive measures.

John Hely-Hutchinson (1757–1832) was the 2nd Earl of Donoughmore. In 1798, when the French, under Humbert, landed in Killala Bay in County Sligo with fifteen thousand men, John Hely-Hutchinson was in command at Castlebar. Frightened by the threatening size of Humbert's forces, the Irish Militia under General Lake and Cornwallis took to the fields and ran. Despite this embarrassing debacle, dubbed by the natives, 'The Races of Castlebar', Hely-Hutchinson retained his command. He soldiered in Egypt and carved out a

John Hely-Hutchinson (1724–1794), Provost of Trinity College, Dublin

distinguished career. He was a friend of George IV who sent him on a mission to St. Omer to offer an allowance of £50,000 a year to Queen Caroline, who was disporting herself there. The conditions were that she relinquished all British royal titles and never visited England again. His mission was not successful.

The two outstanding artists in the Healy family are quite opposite. G. P. A. Healy (1813–1894), a portrait painter, was born in Boston, the eldest son of William Healy, a sea captain of Irish descent and his wife, Mary Hicks. He studied for some years in Paris where he painted Louis Philippe and other French notables. When he returned to America he painted three of the series of United States Presidents; John Tyler (1841–1845), James Knox Polk (1845–1849) and Zachary Taylor (1849–1850).

Michael Healy (1873–1941), a Dublin man, was an artist in stained glass. Richard Hayward, the writer of Irish travel books, described his work in the modern Dominican Holy Cross church in Tralee, County Kerry, as 'exquisite . . . carried out in the most masterly style'. Hayward wrote that his genius was 'traditional and reflective in spirit'.

Timothy Healy (1855–1931), born in Bantry, County Cork, was the son of Maurice Healy, a clerk of the Bantry union. His mother's father, a Sullivan, was a schoolmaster; her three brothers became Members of Parliament, as did her three sons of whom Timothy was the outstanding character. They were the foundations of an Irish political grouping named the 'Bantry Band'.

Tim Healy began to earn his living at thirteen in England, but moved quickly into the political and literary world. He became firmly established as a politician when Charles Stewart Parnell invited him to become his secretary. An audacious politician, in time he developed into a fearless speaker in the House of Commons in the cause of various Irish improvements, especially land ownership. When the split against Parnell began, Healy turned completely against him.

As a member of the English Bar he took on many cases of a political nature and he defended a number of the suffragettes. His wit and eloquence always drew crowded houses, especially when he made biting comments about the Nationalist party. He supported Britain in World War I, but the events of 1916 drove him homewards. After the Treaty he became the first Governor-General of the Irish Free State, a post he filled most successfully from 1922 until 1927.

Tim Healy (1855–1931), colourful politician and first Governor General of the Irish Free State

John Edward Healy was born in Drogheda, County Louth. A prizeman in prose and verse at Trinity College, Dublin, he followed a career in journalism. In 1896 he began with the *Daily Express* of which he later became editor. One of the most outstanding journalists of his era, John Healy was editor of the *Irish Times* from 1907 until his death in 1934—a period of great significance in Irish history.

Gerard Healy (1918–1963) was born in Dublin where he made his name as an actor at the Gate and Abbey theatres and on television. He wrote two plays, *Thy Dear Father* (1943) and *The Black Stranger* (1945) which were both popular at the Abbey Theatre. While playing James Joyce, the leading part in Hugh Leonard's *Stephen D*, in London, he died suddenly.

HENNESSY

I T is seldom if ever that O' is used to prefix Hennessy. In Irish it is O hAonghusa, which signifies descent through Aonghus or Angus, an authentic Gaelic name. There were at least four Hennessy septs spread out over Leinster and Munster, and there are a number of places called Ballyhennessy in Clare, Cork and Kerry.

The principal Hennessy family had their stronghold in north Offaly where they shared the lordship of Clan Cholgain with the O'Holohans. Another branch of the Hennessys lived west of Dublin where the river Liffey runs between the counties of Meath and Dublin. After the Norman invasion they were dispersed and they spread south to Cork, Limerick and Tipperary where most of the Hennessys are to be found at the present day. Hensey or Henchy are variants of the name.

It is in comparatively recent times that the Hennessys who remained in Ireland have come to the fore. They were, of course, very prominent abroad, especially in the service of France.

Henry Hennessy (1826–1901), a Cork born scientist, was a Professor of Engineering in the new Catholic University in Dublin. He was devoted to mathematics and physics and he contributed many writings to learned societies. He was also Professor of Applied Mathematics at the Royal College of Science and Vice-President of the Royal Irish Academy.

William Maunsell Hennessy (1829–1889) came from Castlegregory, County Kerry. An Irish scholar and patriot, he was on the staff of *The Nation*, the newspaper founded by the Young Irelanders. He worked in the Public Record Office and edited many learned papers on Irish history, including the *Annals of Lough Ce*.

The parents of William John Hennessy (1839–1917) fled from their native Kilkenny to Canada, following the abortive rising of the Young Ireland party. They moved to New York where William John Hennesy studied art. Soon his paintings were selling extremely well. However, it was as an illustrator he made his name. He was described as 'a predestined graphic laureate'; he illustrated the books of poetry published by the leading Victorian poets, Tennyson, Longfellow, Whitton, Stedman, Browning. He was elected an Academician in 1863. When he went to England he exhibited regularly at the Royal Academy and he spent much of his later years travelling about France and England.

Sir John Pope Hennessy (1834–1891) was born in Cork where he studied Law and in 1859 he became an M.P. for Westmeath, the first Catholic Conservative member to hold an Irish seat. In 1867 he began his long series of colonial governorships; in Labuan: the Gold Coast where he took over Fort Elmina from the Dutch: the Windward Islands: Barbados: Hong Kong: Mauritius: the Bahamas. He was knighted in 1880, though he was far from popular with his official colleagues because of his impulsive initiating of reforms. He sowed the seeds of colonial independence wherever he went. The worst they could say of him was, 'His failure as a governor was due to want of tact and judgement, and his facility for initiating where he might conciliate'.

In 1890, on his retirement from the British colonial service, he bought Rostellan in Youghal, County Cork, the former home of Sir Walter Raleigh. He contested North Kilkenny as an anti-Parnellite Home Ruler. He carried the seat despite all Parnell's counter efforts. Ironically, the effort was too great for both men; they died that year, within a few hours of each other.

At Kilavullen, seven miles from Mallow, County Cork, on a cliff overhanging the river, is the house in which lived the ancestors of the famous Hennessy family known internationally for their association with brandy. This association came about when, in 1740, Richard Hennessy, third son of Charles Hennessy of Ballymacmoy, County Cork, settled in France. One of the 'Wild Geese', he was an officer in Dillon's Regiment in the service of Louis XV. He fought at Fontenoy and was a wounded veteran when he settled in Cognac, choosing it because it was near where his old comrades of the Irish Brigade were stationed.

Richard Hennessy, captain in the Irish Brigade in France, and founder of the famous brandy business

81

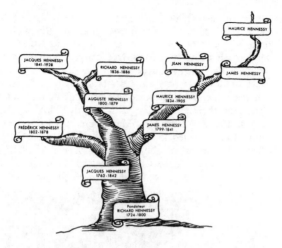

Hearing that the local brandy had restorative powers, he tried it and sent some casks to his friends in Ireland. Their response was wildly enthusiastic. He decided to go into the business and, in 1765, founded a company which was later re-formed by James, his son.

James Hennessy, although he never became naturalized, was accepted as a member of the French Chamber of Deputies and became a peer of France, and he married into the established brandy family of Martell.

Two Irish characteristics the Hennessys brought with them abroad were the appreciation of good liquor and good horseflesh. Their business took them frequently to England and the Hennessys were among the first to sponsor a steeplechase in England. The Hennessy Gold Cup still features largely in the racing calendar. 'Gainsborough', a horse from the Hennessy stable, won the Triple Crown, and no French-owned horse had won the Grand National until Hennessy's 'Lutteur II' won it in 1909.

In France the Hennessy line remains unbroken and, in their list of directors, Maurice, Patrick and Kilian, testify to their adherence to ancestral names.

A collateral branch of the Hennessys, based in England, retains strong links by marriage, commerce or politics with both France and Ireland. George Richard James Hennessy, 1st Baron Windlesham, was created a baronet in 1927 and was created a peer in 1937. He served with many distinctions in the first World War and was a Minister for Labour and a Vice-Chamberlain of the Household.

The 3rd Lord Windlesham, David J. G. Hennessy (1932) has been Minister for State in the Home Office and has held a number of appointments in English regional television companies.

Through the centuries Hennessys have frequently filled the ecclesiastical records. In the 1480's, Nicholas O'Hennessy was a Bishop of Waterford and Lismore. In the last century, John Hennessy of Bulgaden, County Limerick, the eldest of eight children, went to America where he was ordained at Carendalet, St. Louis, Mo. In 1866 he became Bishop of Dubuque, the first archbishop of that state. He devoted himself to the enlargement of education and he died in America in 1900.

KAVANAGH

K AVANAGH, sometimes Cavanagh, is an anglicization of Caomhanach, an adjective denoting association with St. Caomhan. There were several St. Caomhans, and one of them, who was also known as St. Kevin, was foster father to Donal who became the first Kavanagh. The Kavanagh surname has never had the prefix O' or Mac.

Donal was the natural son of the most unpopular man in Irish history, Dermot MacMurrough, King of Leinster about 1126, who, enmeshed in a power struggle with the other provincial kings, put an end to Ireland's independence by inviting its take-over by the Normans. For an inducement he offered his well-endowed daughter, Eva, as bride to Richard, Earl of Pembroke, known as Strongbow—there is an effigy of him in Dublin's Christ Church.

Dermot MacMurrough, renowned for his opportunism and his savagery in war, was not averse to amorous diversions. At one time he had abducted, seemingly not too unwillingly, Dervorgilla the beautiful wife of Tiernan O'Ruairc, Lord of Breifne, but seems to have returned her fairly speedily.

Dermot, a man of many parts, was sometimes a patron of religion and learning. Although he sacked abbeys, he also founded them. In his castle at Ferns in Wexford, once the finest of its kind, he kept one of the splendid books of Irish literature, the *Book of Leinster*.

Not for long did he enjoy his Norman guests. In 1171, the year after their arrival, he died suddenly. He is reputed to be buried in the Cistercian Abbey of Vallis Salutis which he founded outside the town of Baltinglass in County Wicklow, though some historians think he may have been buried at Ferns.

Irish kingship was not hereditary and though Donal was MacMurrough's favourite son he did not follow in his father's footsteps. However, he appears to have come into vast territories in Counties Wexford and Carlow where, until recently, the Kavanaghs were extensive landowners. Kavanagh, particularly in these areas, is one of the most numerous of Irish names.

Art MacMurrough Kavanagh (1357–1417) reigned for forty-two years as King of Leinster and he waged incessant war against the English invaders who had deprived him of his land. He was particularly active against Richard II. In fact, it was partly because of these continual engagements abroad with Ireland that Richard II lost his throne to Henry IV. Art MacMurrough Kavanagh continued to do battle against every English envoy until he died in his sixtieth year. It was suspected he had been poisoned—the only way that could be found to quell this fierce warrior. He is buried at New Ross, County Wexford.

In 1540 Cahir MacMurrough Kavanagh, the Kavanagh chieftain, was induced by the English Deputy, Sir Anthony St. Leger, to renounce the MacMurrough prefix and to promise that 'in future no one should be elected chief but they would obey the King's law and hold their lands by knight-service and accept such rules as the King should appoint', thus ending the MacMurrough kingship. For this submission Cahir was created a baron.

In the seventeenth century many of the Kavanaghs had gone abroad to fight for the Stuart cause. In the army of King James, Brian Kavanagh was remarkable because he was the tallest man of all.

Morgan Kavanagh fled from Ireland after the Treaty of Limerick in 1691. He, too, was a remarkably large man—few men in Europe could equal him in stature. Apart from his physical endowments he also became a man of affairs in Europe, becoming Governor of Prague in 1766.

Kavanaghs were officers in the Irish Brigades in the French army, but it was in the service of Austria that they were most numerous.

Joseph Kavanagh played a prominent and most ignoble part in the French Revolution. A bootmaker, he was chosen as one of the citizens to talk to the representatives of the sixty Paris municipal districts about the formation of a bourgeois National Guard. Kavanagh, with a few citizens, looted the Guard house of the Tuileries and, next morning, seized more guns and urged the citizens to attack the Bastille. It fell as the result of an apparently spontaneous rising, but later it emerged that Joseph Kavanagh was probably one of a number of panic-mongers employed by the Orleanist conspirators.

In 1791 he was a police inspector in Paris, and in 1792 he was one of the

Julia Kavanagh, novelist and writer (1824–1877)

brutal gang who butchered fifteen hundred defenceless men and women at the prison of La Force. In the following Reign of Terror he is mentioned as raiding Royalist homes, arresting people, putting seals on their papers and effects. As a police officer he was also connected with the investigation of the assassination of Marat. The wheel turned full circle when he arrested Philippe Egalité, the Duke of Orleans. After the revolutionary years Joseph Kavanagh disappeared ignominiously.

In Ireland, in the troubled times of 1798, the Reverend Father Francis Kavanagh was one of the leaders of the insurrection in County Wexford.

During the same period, Walter Cavanagh had his house in Borris, County Carlow, attacked by the peasantry who thought it contained arms. It was defended by some of the Donegal Militia who fired down from the upper windows. Compared to the disruption wrought on other mansions with their pictures, books, silver and other irreplaceable testaments to history, Walter Cavanagh's house appears to have got off lightly. It had been designed by

Sir Richard Morrison, a notable Irish architect and a pupil of the great Gandon.

Morgan Kavanagh, born about 1800 in Tipperary, wrote novels and poetry and was regarded as an eccentric. In literature he was far outstripped by his daughter Julia Kavanagh (1824–1877). She spent part of her youth in Paris and London and wrote many novels and was one of the earliest women travel writers. She died in Nice.

There were two other Kavanagh women writing, mostly poetry, towards the close of the nineteenth century, Ethna Kavanagh, and Rose Kavanagh, the Tyrone poetess who was born in 1859 in Killadry, near Beragh.

One of the most outstanding of the Kavanagh men, Arthur MacMurrough Kavanagh (1831–1889) was a son of Thomas Kavanagh, M.P. He was a Borris, County Carlow, Kavanagh who could trace his ancestry from the kings of Leinster. Although Arthur MacMurrough Kavanagh was born with only the rudiments of arms and legs, he rode fearlessly, he fished and shot, drew and wrote. He travelled extensively and hazardously in Europe and the East with his brothers who died from various mishaps, leaving him heir.

He married and had a large family. He was a philanthropist, a good landlord and a county magistrate. He was both Conservative and Protestant and he sat in Parliament for County Wexford and, later, for County Carlow. He did not agree with the disestablishment of the Irish church but he supported the Land Act of 1870. He was a member of the Privy Council in Ireland. A number of books and stories have been written about this brave and brilliant Kavanagh.

In modern times the quirky country poet, Patrick Kavanagh (1906–1967) is the Kavanagh of stature. Born in Monaghan he grew up on the farm and his poetry stemmed from the Gaelic tradition. He became a major Irish poet, the most important for many years. Latterly he disapproved of his most popular poem, *The Great Hunger*, written in 1942. He is represented in all the major anthologies and his two novels, *The Green Fool* and *Tarry Flynn* are regarded as classics.

In much earlier days Eileen, who was daughter of a Kavanagh chieftain, is said to have inspired the great thirteenth-century poet, Carol O'Daly, to compose the well-known song, *Eileen Aroon*, with its haunting air.

The Castle of Enniscorthy, once the stronghold of the Wexford Kavanaghs, has passed through many hands and is now a very interesting folk museum. Among the many ruined monasteries which enrich the haunting atmosphere of the Irish countryside, are a number which were built by the Kavanaghs, especially in the adjoining counties of Carlow, Wicklow and Wexford. The Kavanagh drinking horn made of ivory and ornamented with gilt metal plates and bands, stands sixteen inches high.

The Kavanagh drinking horn

O'KEEFFE

THE Irish forename from which this County Cork sept took their name was Caomh. Art Caemh was the son of the King of Munster who was slain in 902. In Norman times the O'Keeffes, in Irish O'Caoimh, were chased from one part of County Cork to the other. So many of them settled in the Duhallow region of West Cork that the area acquired the lasting name of Pobal O'Keeffe. To this day the O'Keeffe name is prominent all over County Cork.

Father Eoghan (Owen) O'Keeffe (1656–1726), of Glenville, was president of the bards of North Cork. A Gaelic poet of considerable achievement he entered the church after the death of his wife. He was parish priest of Doneraile until his death at the age of seventy. Many of his songs are still to be heard in rural districts.

O'Keeffes were amongst the many families driven into exile. Constantine O'Keeffe (1671–1745), the intrepid officer of the Irish Brigade, was admitted into the nobility of France. For this rare honour he must either have been able to prove a long and very aristocratic Irish lineage, or to have shown great bravery and brilliant strategy on the battlefield. General Patrick O'Keeffe (1740–1809), some generations later, was also with the Irish Brigade in which he actively served for forty-seven years despite being severely wounded at least four times.

The O'Keeffes came frequently to the fore as painters and dramatists. Daniel O'Keeffe (1740–1786), was Dublin born and he trained at the Dublin Society's drawing school where he won several prizes. He went to London to establish himself and, during his thirties, began to exhibit at the Royal Academy. This success gave him the confidence to restore the Gaelic 'O' to his surname. His brother John, the dramatist, had already said, 'Few of us old Irish ventured to sport our "O"s at that period.' Daniel was stricken by consumption and died at the early age of forty-six.

His brother, John (1747–1833), was a most prolific writer who contributed to nearly every aspect of comic drama. He had also studied at the Dublin Society's art school, but he developed a taste for the stage. He made his debut as an actor at the Smock Alley Theatre in Dublin in a comedy written by himself. He acted for a dozen years with considerable success, but when still quite young he became almost totally blind. He moved to London where he managed to find his outlet in writing, assisted by his daughter, Adelaide, who was a novelist and writer of historical romances.

John O'Keeffe's plays and songs were so popular they were in the repertories all over Britain until comparatively recently. Yet a critic has described his turn of phrase as being 'a contrivance of significant gibberish'. He was responsible for *Amo, Amas, I loved a Lass*, and the famous song, *I am a Friar of Orders Grey*, from his comic opera *Merry Sherwood*. His plays in prose and verse included such great favourites as *Tony Lumpkin in Town* and *The Castle of Andalusia*, and *Wild Oats*, all written in the last half of the eighteenth century. In 1798 he published a collection of his comedies and farces which ran to four volumes. In 1826 his *Recollections* were published and he died a few years afterwards in Southampton.

Mrs. John O'Keeffe, painted by her husband

He had been awarded a Royal pension. His portrait by Thomas Lawrenson, painted in 1786, was hung in London's National Portrait Gallery.

Another John O'Keeffe, little known today, was a painter of a different genre from Daniel, his antecedent. Born at Fermoy, County Cork, in 1797, he was apprenticed to a coach painter. He developed into a skilled heraldic artist. In Cork he adopted portrait painting and many altar pieces by his brush can be discovered in that neighbourhood. He exhibited at the Royal Hibernian Academy, but he died in 1838 before he had sufficient time to develop.

A sentence of two years for making a seditious speech would be unthinkable today, but that was what John O'Keeffe, a member of Dail Eireann for North Cork, was given for making such a speech in 1919.

KELLY (O'Kelly, Kelley)

K ELLY is the second most numerous surname in Ireland, only surpassed by the Murphys. Tadg Mor Ó'Ceallaigh was killed at the battle of Clontarf in 1014. His name came from Ceallach (the Irish for war or contention), a name belonging to several distinct families. The enfield, that strange heraldic beast borne by some branches of the O'Kelly family, is said to have had its origins at Clontarf when it came out of the sea to protect Tadg Mor's body until his kinsmen arrived to give their chief suitable burial.

The O'Kellys were one of the most powerful families in Connacht where they ruled over eighty thousand acres as chiefs of Ui Maine, the present Galway and Roscommon, at one time known as 'O'Kelly's Country'. The Abbey of Kilconnell, seven miles from Ballinasloe, County Galway, was founded in 1400 by an O'Kelly and the enfield can be seen on many of the tombstones there. Traces of their castles can be found at Aughrim, Garbally, Gallagh, Monivea, Moylough, Mullaghmore, Castlekelly and Screen—a most important manor; the 10th and last Lord of Screen, Captain Denis O'Kelly, died there in 1740.

There were eight other distinct O'Kelly families. The more prominent ones were lords of Breagh, a large part of present-day Meath and north County Dublin. The Cinel Eachach O'Kellys are still to be found at Derry. There were also O'Kelly chieftains in Leix, Wicklow, Sligo and Cork. The events of history have dispersed the O'Kellys far and wide and they have long been established in Europe, Britain, Australia, and America north and south.

At the Royal Irish Academy in Dublin, *The Book of the O'Kellys* is preserved. Written in the fourteenth century it shows an awareness of contemporary history, synchronizing the reigns of Roman Emperors and Irish kings. It was compiled by a bishop of Clonfert, Murtough O'Kelly, afterwards archbishop of Tuam, who had four sons, an accepted situation at that time. His son, Thomas, who died in 1441, succeeded to his father's bishopric.

Daniel O'Kelly who lived in the middle of the thirteenth century was the first Dominican priest to become an Irish bishop. Ralph Kelly of Drogheda, as archbishop of Cashel, defended the rights of the church against the parliament held at Kilkenny in 1342. St. Grellan, a contemporary of St. Patrick's, was the patron saint of the O'Kellys, and his crozier, lost comparatively recently, was always used as their battle standard. Unfortunately, they were too much inclined to battle, not only against the invading Norman and British, but among themselves also. Nonetheless, historians regard the expansion of the O'Kellys in Connacht as one of the most remarkable features of the close of the fourteenth century.

They were also noted for their hospitality. In 1351, O'Kelly, chief of Ui Maine, sent an invitation to all the poets, musicians and artists of Ireland to feast with him at Christmas. This feast earned the poetic description 'the welcome of all welcomes', and ever since 'O'Kelly's Welcome' has come to mean great hospitality.

Malachy O'Kelly, who succeeded to the chieftaincy of Ui Maine in 1499, was so enraged when his newly built castles at Monivea and Garbally were destroyed by Clanrickard, that he called on Garret Mor, the great Earl of Kildare, to help him get his revenge. All the principal chiefs, O'Donnell, O'Neill, McMahon,

O'Hanlon, Magennis, O'Reilly, O'Farrell, joined in. Gunpowder was used for the first time and at Knocktoe, near Galway, the opposing forces, combining the O'Briens, McNamaras, O'Carrolls, O'Kennedys, led by Ulick Burke, Earl of Clanrickard, were horribly defeated. It was in reality an inter-family quarrel, but it contributed significantly to the later downfall of native Irish supremacy.

John O'Kelly, 8th lord of the manor of Screen, County Galway, educated his son Charles (1621–1695) at St. Omer in France. In 1642 he returned to the aid of Ormond, the Lord Lieutenant, who was steering a difficult course between the Catholic and Old English Confederates at Kilkenny and Charles II of England. When Charles II was executed and Cromwell came to devastate Ireland, Charles O'Kelly and many of his kinsmen went to Spain. At the restoration, Colonel Charles O'Kelly, though sixty-eight years old, returned to Connacht and fought at Aughrim. After the siege of Limerick he retired to Castle Kelly where he died in 1695. He left behind an extraordinary manuscript which continues to puzzle the historians. Known as the 'Macariae Excidium' it is a translation from a supposed work which Charles O'Kelly put into English. In fact it seems to be Charles O'Kelly himself, heavily disguised, giving a straightforward account of the struggle in Ireland between James II and William III.

The O'Kellys have shaped the course of history in curious ways. It is suspected that it was an O'Kelly who fired the gun that killed Garret Mor, the Great Earl of Kildare, in 1513. And it seems that it was Daniel O'Kelly who murdered the great Earl of Desmond in 1583, near Tralee, and delivered the head to Ormond who sent it to Queen Elizabeth where it was spiked on London Bridge.

The O'Kellys also have to acknowledge Colla Kelly who fought on the English side in the tragic battle of Kinsale in 1601. Kinsale left the Irish no choice but to flee abroad, and they joined all the different regiments of the Irish Brigade. The O'Kelly name began to appear in France, Austria, Spain and Belgium. The O'Kellys of Belgium are descendants of Captain John O'Kelly of Galway who advised the Austrian Emperor on the government of his army.

Count William O'Kelly was also with the Austrian Emperor, as Knight of Arms.

Father Malachy O'Kelly in 1684 founded the Irish College in Paris. A Count O'Kelly was the Minister Plenipotentiary of France at the Court of the Elector of Mayence at the time of the revolution. A Major O'Kelly, at the age of seventy, fought with the French army in the Vendean war.

By the eighteenth century, for the O'Kellys at home, there was little fighting. They channelled their energy and talents into literature, the arts in general, and sport. Many of them dropped the Irish prefix and became plain Kelly.

Hugh Kelly (1739–1777), was born in Killarney, and went to England where he worked first as a stay-maker and then found his niche as a journalist and, later, as dramatist. False Delicacy, a comedy, was produced by Garrick and was a great success; so much so that it was translated into the leading European languages. He never reached such heights again and while he was studying law as a more rewarding alternative to authorship, he died suddenly aged only thirty-seven.

Patrick O'Kelly (1754–1835) born in Loughrea, County Galway, earned a seemingly undeserved reputation as a poet—when George IV visited Ireland O'Kelly was presented to him. Eccentric would be a more apt description of his poems, one of which, the famous Doneraile Litany consists of innumerable curses directed at that village and its people because there he lost his watch and chain.

Another Patrick, born in the same year in Dublin, Patrick Kelly, became a noted mathematician and astronomer. In 1813 the House of Commons consulted him on currency questions. He was eighty-six when he died in Brighton.

Catherine Kelly (1756–1785) was known in her brief life as 'the Irish fairy'. She was only thirty-four inches tall and weighed but twenty-two pounds.

Micheal Kelly who was born in Dublin about 1764 was a child prodigy who could play complicated piano pieces at eleven years. He was sent for training to Naples with an introduction to Sir William Hamilton. He trained as a tenor and travelled all over Europe—Mozart wrote Basilio specially for him in *The Marriage of Figaro*. For a while he sang and composed in London with great success because of his wide musical background. He seems to have abandoned his music when he returned to look after his father's wine business. He fitted many roles into his sixty odd years.

Dennis Kelly, born in Ireland early in the eighteenth century, went to London to make his fortune, and did so after he managed to buy the famous racehorse 'Eclipse'. He made his wealth from horse dealing and he travelled up the social scale by getting himself a commission in the Middlesex militia. He left a lot of money and a clause in his will that his heir must forfeit £400 for every bet he made. He died in his Piccadilly house in London in 1787.

Captain John Kelly who inspired the rousing ballad, *Kelly the boy from Killann*, was born in that village in County Wexford and met his death leading the insurgents at New Ross in 1798.

Mary Eva Kelly, born in Headford, County Galway, married the fiery Young Irelander, Kevin Izod O'Doherty. She wrote nationalistic poems and essays for *The Nation*, the newspaper published by the Young Irelanders, and became known as 'Eva of The Nation'. She lived until 1910.

In the last hundred years the number of Kellys who have been writers, dramatists, journalists, causes considerable confusion. J. J. O'Kelly (1873–1957) distinguished himself by writing many books on Irish history using the name 'Sceilg'. He was a language revival enthusiast, a President of the Gaelic League and he succeeded Eamon De Valera as President of Sinn Fein. Seamus O'Kelly (1881–1920) came from Loughrea to Dublin to work as a journalist and was caught up in the revolutionary movement which culminated in the rising of 1916. His plays were produced at the Abbey Theatre, Dublin. A radio version of his short story, *The Weaver's Grave*, won the Italia Prize in 1961.

James Plunkett Kelly was born in Dublin the year Seamus O'Kelly died. He worked first as a trades union official, then went into radio and television as a producer. When he began to write his plays and novels he dropped the Kelly and as James Plunkett is the author of the best-selling novel, *Strumpet City*, set in Dublin during the infancy of trade unionism before the first world war.

Seán T. O'Ceallaigh, a Dublin man (1882–1966) was President of Ireland for fourteen years. In 1905 he was one of the founder members of the Sinn Fein party and he took an active part in the struggle for independence from Britain. He was Speaker in the first Dáil, the Irish Parliament, and held many ministerial offices.

The Kellys abroad are as numerous as in the country from which they emigrated. They are in Canada, in South America, and in the United States the Kellys and their counterparts, the Cohens, have become part of folk history.

KELLY

The first bishop of Richmond, Virginia, in 1820, was Patrick Kelly (1779–1829) who was born in Kilkenny.

Colonel Patrick Kelly commanded the Irish Brigade at the battle of Gettysburg in 1863. Michael Kelly (1857–1894), was the U.S. baseball champion of his time. Edgar Stilman Kelley (1857–1944) combined two of the Kelly characteristics, musical composition and writing. In 1886 the leader of Tammany Hall was 'Honest' John Kelly. Tammany Hall was the New York headquarters of the Democratic Party. It became predominantly Irish and had an unsavoury record for corruption.

There were Kelly millionaires. Thomas Hughes Kelly (1865–1933), a banker's son, was a philanthropist who continued his father's support for the struggle for independence in the old country.

Sean T. O'Kelly (1882–1966), politician and President of Ireland for fourteen years

John Henry Kelly (1857–1944) left Mayo an unskilled labourer and made his money in insurance. He had six sons, one of whom was Jack, the greatest oarsman in the United States in the twenties. He later became a millionaire building contractor and was the father of the film actress Grace Kelly who became Princess Grace of Monaco. His brother George, a Pullitzer prize winner, wrote two very successful plays, *Craig's Wife* and *Show Off*. This family was known collectively as 'The Kellys of Philadelphia'.

Captain Colin Kelly was the first great hero of the second world war.

The Kellys in Australia range from Michael Kelly (1850–1940), Bishop of Sydney, to Ned Kelly the gangster leader who was hanged in Melbourne in 1880

91

Grace Kelly (Princess Grace) with her husband Prince Rainier of Monaco paying one of their regular visits to Ireland

and is now inspiring writers, film and television producers with his saga of unhappy social history.

Sir David Kelly (1891–1959) could be counted as a Kelly who returned. Born in Adelaide, he returned to the land of his parents and entered the British diplomatic service in 1919. He was British Ambassador in Moscow from 1949 to 1951 and he has written a number of books on his various postings.

In the last edition of Burke's Landed Gentry of Ireland, dated 1958, five O'Kelly families are separately listed. One of these families, formerly of Gallagh in County Galway, had an ancestor, Dillon John (1766–1811) who distinguished himself in the Austrian imperial service. He died childless and his nephew was granted his title of Count by Maria Theresa with the proviso that it 'may be borne by all descendants in the male line'. The daughters could be countesses but they could not transmit the imperial title to their issue.

In modern times there have been many Counts O'Kelly de Gallagh distinguished in the service of diplomacy, the army, the arts and commerce.

KENNEDY

I T seems there are Kennedys who could call themselves relations of Brian Boru. There are also Scottish Kennedys, but the Irish Kennedys derive their descent from Cinnéide, or, in English, Kennedy, nephew of Brian Boru the victor of the battle of Clontarf. They owned extensive territory around Glenomra and Killaloe in County Clare where there is still an area called Killokennedy. When they were ousted by the powerful O'Briens and MacNamaras they settled in Tipperary. Here they became numerous and strong again and from the twelfth to the sixteenth century they ranked as Lords of Ormond. They divided into three branches: The Fionn (fair) Kennedys, The Don (brown) Kennedys and the Rua (red) Kennedys. The colour of the hair was a great distinguishing feature of the ancient Irish.

The Kennedys managed to grapple with the various conquests and confiscations more successfully than many other Gaelic families. However, through the centuries many of them went abroad. In Spain, for example, Kennedy and Quenedy are one and the same name.

Matthew (1652–1735) was one of the Kennedys who went to France in 1691 after the disastrous siege of Limerick by the army of William III. Matthew Kennedy settled in Paris where he became a notable literary figure and was undoubtedly a linguist for he managed also to keep up an active interest in his native Irish.

In 1779 a strange case came before the Irish courts when two Miss Kennedys, daughters of a wealthy County Waterford family, were abducted. It was not altogether unheard of in those days for daring young men of high fashion but little means to attempt to improve their finances in this very forceful fashion.

The Reverend John Kennedy, an Ulster Presbyterian, possibly a Scots Kennedy, has left a diary giving an interesting account of the social history of the mid-eighteenth century.

Patrick Kennedy (1801–1871) who was born in Wexford established himself in Dublin as a bookseller and published popular books of Irish legends and folk tales. In the United States of America the Irish-American, Patrick John Kennedy (1843–1906) specialized in Catholic publications.

At the beginning of the nineteenth century the Reverend James Kennedy was a notable classical scholar and a Fellow of Trinity College, Dublin. He died in County Tyrone where he was Rector of Ardtrea.

Sir Arthur Kennedy (1810–1883) came from Cultra, County Down, and was also a Trinity College graduate. He retired from the army in 1848, the time of the famine, and he did his duty as a Poor Law Inspector. In 1851 he began a very varied series of colonial governorships. First he went to the Gambia, then to Western Australia. He was knighted in 1868 and was afterwards Governor of Hong Kong and then of Queensland.

Evory Kennedy of the same generation as Sir Arthur, was born at Carndonagh, County Derry. He studied medicine first in Dublin, then Edinburgh, London and Paris, and became one of the most popular of Dublin medical men. He was appointed Master of the Rotunda—the second oldest lying-in hospital in the world. In 1833 he was President of the College of Surgeons, Dublin. As home-ruler he contested Donegal but was not so successful as a politician. He died in London.

The Irish Free State, which was founded in 1922 had, as its first Chief Justice, Hugh Kennedy (1879–1936).

The tragic Kennedy family of America whose sons for a decade dominated the political scene there came originally from a County Wexford farming family.

John F. Kennedy with the former president of the Irish Republic, Eamon de Valera

President John FitzGerald Kennedy visited Ireland a year before his assassination and spent a while in the ancestral cottage at Dunganstown, taking tea with his Kennedy kinsmen. The vitality of his short spell as President of the U.S.A. brought a reflected glory to Ireland, where his violent death, and that of his sister and brothers was very keenly felt.

The Kennedy surname is widely distributed over Ireland and is very numerous. It holds sixteenth place in the statistical list of Irish surnames, which might account for about twenty thousand Irish Kennedys.

KEOGH
(MacKeogh, Kehoe, O'Hoey, Hoy)

K EOGH is so thoroughly Gaelic that only the Irish can get their tongue easily around its proper pronunciation. Kee-oh is approximately how it is pronounced. Originally it was Eochaidh, even more difficult to enunciate. Their ancestry is said to come from Eochaidh O'Kelly. There were three branches of the family. Ballymackeogh in County Tipperary was the territory of one sept. The lords of Magh Finn—their territory of Moyfinn was around Athlone in County Roscommon—belonged to the second branch. A part of this area was known as Keoghville until quite recent times.

Historically the most important was the third sept, the MacKeoghs of Leinster. They were of the same stock as the O'Byrnes to whom they were also hereditary bards. In medieval times, after the Anglo-Norman invasion, they moved with the O'Byrnes and the O'Tooles across the plains of County Kildare to the protection of the Wicklow mountains, and also south to Wexford. Maolmuire MacKeogh is described by The Four Masters as the chief professor of poetry in Leinster in 1534. In his *Literary History of Ireland* Douglas Hyde mentions several poets of the name.

Literature and, later, politics, seem to be their medium. The Reverend John

John Keogh (1740–1817), early campaigner for Catholic Emancipation

95

Keogh, a Protestant clergyman whose property was confiscated in the Cromwellian wars, was a noted scholar. Born at Cloondeagh, Limerick, in 1653, he wrote Latin verse. His mathematical demonstration of religious problems was admired by Sir Isaac Newton. His eldest son, John (1681–1754), made his name as a botanist and zoologist.

There were three prominent politicians. Matthew Keogh (1744–1798), was hanged for the part he played in the 1798 insurrection.

In the Penal days, before Daniel O'Connell campaigned for Catholic emancipation, John Keogh (1740–1817) had also begun to work towards this objective.

William Keogh (1817–1878), born at Keoghville, near Galway, is regarded as a renegade. He graduated in Law from Trinity College, Dublin. He was a Catholic Liberal M.P. for Athlone and was made a Q.C. and appointed Solicitor General in 1852. Speaking out against extreme nationalism he gave great offence and was denounced as an oathbreaker. In 1856 he was a judge and as a member of an old Gaelic family it should have gone against the grain for him to act as judge at the Fenian trials of 1865. It did not and he tried and sentenced the Fenians. For this he has never been forgiven and his effigy was burned as a traitor. He became discredited and when it was also discovered that he had been an associate of the swindler, Sadleir, he fled the country. Keogh retired to Bingen on the Rhine where, possibly in a fit of madness, he made a murderous attack on his valet and afterwards slit his own throat.

Captain Myles Keogh, killed at the Battle of Little Bighorn

There was a Keogh at the battle of Little Bighorn against the Sioux Indians in 1876. He was Captain Myles Keogh who lost his life fighting in this battle in which every one of the U.S. forces was killed and only Keogh's horse survived the animal slaughter.

During the 1914–1918 war, Sir Alfred Keogh was Director General of the Army Medical Services. On the Eastern front he became interested in the cause and cure of malaria which had so much afflicted the troops. In Britain he set up special malaria hospitals and, with Sir Ronald Ross, promoted the use of quinine for its control.

LYNCH

L YNCH, which is among the most widespread of Irish surnames, has arrived at its present simplification from two different sources.

One was the Norman family of de Lench who became an important member of the famous 'Tribes of Galway'. They provided eighty-four mayors of Galway from 1484, when Dominick Lynch was given its first charter by Richard III, to 1654, when Catholics were debarred from civic offices.

In 1493 the mayor of Galway hanged his own son because he had killed a visiting Spaniard and for that the penalty was death. Beside the church of St. Nicholas in Galway city, on the site of the old jail, there is still standing a doorway with an inscription commemorating the execution of Walter Lynch by his father, James Lynch Fitzstephen. Nearby, at the corner of Shop Street, stands Lynch's Castle, built in 1302, a fine stone mansion which was the home of the Lynch family. Today it houses a bank.

Galway was once a walled town. In those turbulent medieval times it was impossible for a man of means to exist outside a fortified place and he had the choice between a walled town or a castle. Sir Robert Lynch owned Corundalla Castle and Nicholas Lynch owned nearby Annaghdown Castle. Connacht is rich in castles for they were a necessity in the west of Ireland up to a later period than in the greater part of Europe.

In 1566 Dominick Lynch, an enlightened educationist, founded the free school at Galway. There Alexander Lynch gathered twelve hundred scholars from all parts of Ireland and laid the foundations of a great school of classical and Irish learning. And there his son, Dr. John Lynch, a philosopher, had 'the beginnings of his erudition'. Another master, James Lynch, 'gave long, painful, and profitable service . . . in the training and breeding of the children of the members of

Lynch's Castle, Galway city

97

The inscription which commemorates Walter Lynch, executed by his father

this Corporation for the space of thirty years and upwards in good literature and sciences liberal'. In his declining years he was given a recompense of an annuity of £10.

After 1654, and the invasion of Cromwell's army, all this great learning was swept away. The Reverend John Lynch of Galway (1600–1673), an Archdeacon of Tuam, translated Keating's *History* and wrote *Cambrensis Eversus*, one of the most valuable works on Irish history and memoirs, but he was forced to flee to France. From there he wrote: 'I could not bear to return to see reduced to beggary those whose opulence and public spirit has adorned my native town. I cannot exchange the free altars and noble churches of France for the garret churches and flimsy hiding places of Ireland.'

In the Middle Ages trade with Spain and France had flourished from the port of Galway. Many Lynches were educated abroad; some entered the church there. Dominick Lynch of Galway joined the Dominicans at Seville where, in 1674, he was a professor of Theology. Later he presided over the Dominicans in Rome. In Paris he published a large collection of works on philosophy.

Despite imprisonment and poverty, James Lynch (1609–1713), Archbishop of Tuam, managed to administer his diocese, sometimes from abroad, and he lived to the age of one hundred and five. He was one of many distinguished scholar priests of the Lynch family.

Quite distinct from the Galway Norman Lynches, were the Gaelic O'Loinsighs, or Lynches, who comprised a number of different septs, mostly in the Clare, Sligo, Limerick areas, though some branched north to Donegal or south to Cork.

From Sligo came the Dominican Prior of Killaloe (c. 1411), Alan O'Lynch. From Clare, also, came the linguist and Gaelic scholar, Patrick Lynch (1757–1818).

The man who gave his name to the lynch law was Colonel Charles Lynch (1736–1796). He had emigrated to America and appears to have been an administrator of rough justice to those under his command.

One of the signatories of the American Declaration of Independence was a third generation Irishman, Thomas Lynch (1749–1779).

Dr. John Joseph Lynch (1816–1888) emigrated from his native Breifne to become Bishop of Toronto.

Dominick Lynch's wealthy father left Ireland for America towards the close of the eighteenth century. Dominick was educated both in Ireland and in France. As a member of the wine importing business he elevated the social standards in New York. He introduced the chateau-bottled wines of France and was himself an elegant gourmet with a home at Greenwich and an estate in Westchester County. Through his great interest in music his home became one of the focal points for American society. He brought grand opera to the United States—he went himself to Europe to choose an opera company and he looked after them well and helped many musicians and actors, including Fanny Kemble. When he died in 1837 in Paris, Dominick Lynch was mourned as the 'greatest swell and beau New York had ever known'.

In France, a grandson of one of the officers who went abroad with James II after 1691, Count John Baptist Lynch, was almost ruined by the French Revolution, but he managed to get back some of his inheritance. On the other side, General Isadore Lynch joined the revolutionary armies and had a successful military career in the Napoleonic campaigns. And Patrick Lynch (1824–1886) left his Irish home to serve with the British army. He appears to have changed his allegiance for he later became known as Patricio Lynch, 'the foremost Chilean naval hero'.

After the great famine of 1847 there was an Irish colony of Browns, Dillons, Sheridans, Lynches and many others in Buenos Aires. To Paraguay came that colourful and notorious Irish lady, Madame Elizabeth Lynch, with Francisco Lopez II. His father was hereditary dictator of Paraguay, and during the twelve years while her father-in-law was still alive, she lived in regal state in Asuncion and 'showed every hospitality to visitors from Europe'. The wars between Paraguay, the Argentine and Brazil brought this idyll to an end and she accompanied Francisco Lopez II during five years of campaigning until he and their fifteen-year-old son, Francis Lopez, were both killed. Then she surrendered and was treated courteously by the Brazilians, but she left South America and ended her days in England.

A County Mayo family of Lynches became Mesopotamian explorers. Thomas Kerr Lynch (1818–1891) of Partry, Ballinrobe, graduated from Trinity College, Dublin, and joined his brother, Captain Henry Blosse Lynch, in the second Euphrates expedition (1837–1842). Thomas set up a business in Baghdad with a younger brother and they developed a much appreciated steamer service to the interior by way of the river Tigris. For generations the Blosse Lynches have been extensive landowners in the West of Ireland.

Hannah Lynch (1862–1904) of Dublin, at a very tender age took a prominent part in the 'Ladies Land League' which had been formed to counter the evictions resulting from the Land War of the 1880's. Hannah's activities led to her having to flee to France. She took with her the metal type for her Land League publications which she continued printing from Paris. Eventually she settled there and wrote many novels and travel books.

Patricia Lynch (1897–1972) wrote popular children's books which have been translated into many languages. Born in Cork she began work in Dublin as a young journalist, writing first-hand accounts of the 1916 rising. Her best loved book, *The Turf Cutter's Donkey*, was published in 1934 and was illustrated by Jack Yeats.

Patricia Lynch, writer (1897–1972)

Stanislaus Lynch, born in County Cavan in 1907, writes authoritively on hunting and the Irish horse. His works have been translated into many languages and he has received Olympic Diplomas for Literature.

The Lynch family has had many patriots. The most prominent of this century is Liam Lynch (1890–1923). He was very active in the 1916 rising and was a Divisional Commander. He was Chief of Staff of the Republican army during the Civil war and was killed in action against the army of the Free State.

In the 1970's the fierceness of the civil strife in the six counties of northern Ireland has echoed around the world. It has also brought into prominence the name of Jack Lynch, Prime Minister of the Republic from 1966 to 1973. Born in Cork in 1917, he graduated into politics via the law and sport; six successive All-Ireland medals, five for hurling and one for Gaelic football. A barrister and a member of the Fianna Fail party, Jack Lynch was the first Taoiseach (Prime Minister) of the generation which was not actively engaged in the 1916–1922 revolution.

MacMAHON

S O that he could be ennobled by Louis XV in 1763, John Baptist MacMahon (1715–1780) verified his descent from King Brian Boru and received the title Marquis d'Eguilly. He was of the Thomond, or Clare, sept. The other MacMahon sept was of Oriel, the present-day Monaghan and Louth. The Clare MacMahons took their name from Mahon, son of Murtagh More O'Brien, King of Ireland 1094–1119. Corcabaskin, Moyarta, Clonderlaw, were some of their Clare properties. Their last chieftain was slain by his own son—accidentally—after the battle of Kinsale in 1601.

The MacMahons of Monaghan and Louth were once a powerful family in Ulster until scattered south by the disruptions of Elizabethan and Cromwellian wars. Their last great chieftain, Hugh Og (1606–1644) was beheaded at Tyburn. He was married to a daughter of Hugh O'Neill, Earl of Tyrone. With powerful friends he had planned to capture Dublin Castle but was betrayed by a false friend, Owen O'Connolly.

A castle, once a stronghold of the MacMahons, still stands at Carrigaholt, County Clare. In Monaghan there are ruins of the Franciscan friary founded by Phelim MacMahon in 1462.

In the seventeenth century three MacMahons in turn were primates of Armagh. The coats of arms of two of these, the brothers Bernard and Ross MacMahon, are on their gravestones at Edergole in County Monaghan.

The most renowned of the ecclesiastical MacMahons, though he never achieved Armagh, was Heber (1600–1650), son of Turlogh MacMahon. His career was to have been in the Spanish service but his mother, Eva O'Neill, intervened and he went to Douay and was ordained a priest at Louvain. He returned to Ireland and was over forty when appointed bishop of Clogher. A trusted friend of his kinsman, Owen Roe O'Neill, he had his eye on the political situation and eventually joined the Confederate Catholics. In 1650 he was a general in the army of Ulster. Though not versed in military practices he tried a few adventures, mostly disastrous. He was wounded and captured by the English who executed him, not before he had publicly regretted his vain military ambitions.

Hugh MacMahon of County Monaghan, who was appointed Archbishop of Armagh and Primate of Ireland in 1713, wrote a paper confirming the precedence of Armagh over Dublin in matters ecclesiastical. When he died in 1737 he was succeeded by his nephew, Bernard.

Following the Treaty of Limerick in 1691, the defeated Irish army were given the choice of swearing allegiance to William III of England and thereby holding their own property, or of sailing to France in English ships. Of fourteen hundred men only seven chose William, and so France, and Europe, acquired an army of professional soldiers. Romantically dubbed 'the Wild Geese', they were to distinguish themselves in the courts of Europe for generations.

Maurice Francis, son of John Baptist MacMahon, Marquis d'Eguilly, was in the King's army at the outbreak of the French Revolution and was often suspect for his royalist sympathies. He died in 1831, leaving seventeen children.

Carrigaholt Castle in County Clare, once a stronghold of the MacMahons

One of his sons, Edmonde Patrice (1808–1893), like his predecessors, was a professional soldier. He was a general when he had his great victory at Sebastopol, the capture of the Malakoff fortress. It was here, when told it was mined and therefore dangerous, that he made the classic remark: 'J'y suis, j'y reste.' 'Here I am, here I stay.' He survived to become the hero of the Malakoff and Duke of Magenta. In 1873 he was elected President of the Republic of France. This descendant of an Irish royalist family which had followed James II into exile, found it difficult to govern a country so rabidly republican as the France of the 1870s. He resigned in 1879. He died in Paris in 1893 and the Encyclopaedia Britannica describes him as 'a fine, tall soldierly man, of a thoroughly Irish type . . .'

Earlier in France, at the outbreak of the Revolution, there were numerous representatives of the MacMahon family, including an Abbé MacMahon who had once served in the Irish Brigade and was chaplain to the Bastille when it fell.

A Doctor MacMahon, suspected of having royalist sympathies, escaped by pretending to be a member of the Volunteers who were marching to the German frontier. Thoroughly caught up in their campaign he worked in their military hospital. After the Revolution he became physician to the Irish College in Paris and was also Head Librarian at the Paris School of Medicine. In the Paris Archives Nationales there are many references to the Irish MacMahon family in France. The MacMahon sword has been featured several times in *The Irish Sword*, the magazine of the Irish Military History Society.

Thomas O'Brien MacMahon of Tipperary flourished in London in the 1770's when he was writing controversial essays on the general weaknesses of human nature and on the English and Irish natures in particular.

John MacMahon (d.1817) was private secretary and keeper of the privy purse to the Prince Regent, later George IV. He was also a privy councillor and was created a baron in the year he died.

Sir William MacMahon (1776–1837) conformed to Protestantism and studied Law at Trinity College, Dublin. He travelled the Munster circuit with the great Daniel O'Connell. Not a brilliant speaker, he was regarded as a conscientious and fair judge. In 1814 he was made Master of the Rolls and received a baronetcy.

Sir Charles MacMahon (1824–1891), born in Dublin, served in Canada with the 71st Highland Light Infantry, and also in India with the 10th Hussars. When he retired in 1853 he joined the Melbourne police of which he became Chief Commissioner. He was also a member of the Legislative Assembly and was knighted in 1875.

In the United States of America the MacMahons are almost as widespread as in Ireland. Bernard MacMahon (d.1816), left Ireland for political reasons. He settled in Philadelphia where his horticultural nurseries became famous for their rare and exotic plants. Helped by his competent Irish wife he built up one of the biggest seed businesses in the United States. So well-known and popular was he with the prominent botanists and horticulturists of the day that they named a new species of evergreen, *berberis Mahonia*, after him. He had tried, unsuccessfully, to grow vines but he left America its first worthwhile book on horticulture, the *American Gardener's Calendar*.

Also in America John Van Lear McMahon (1800–1871), the son of an Irish Presbyterian farmer and a Maryland mother, graduated from Princeton as a lawyer. His lack of polish was so apparent he returned to his Cumberland home town where he studied medicine and theology. He developed his oratorical powers so thoroughly that he was elected to represent Allegheny County in the Maryland House of Delegates. He became a very successful Maryland lawyer and was active in the construction of the Baltimore and Ohio Railroad. Although he took part in politics he refused to become a candidate for the Senate or to accept a seat in President Harrison's cabinet. He wrote a constitutional history of the government of Maryland. In later years his eyesight failed and he retired from public life.

Bryan MacMahon (1909) of Listowel, County Kerry, is one of Ireland's leading short story writers and playwrights. A Member of the Irish Academy of Letters his plays have been put on at Dublin's Abbey Theatre. He lives at Listowel where he is a teacher.

The historians and scholars are almost agreed that Mahon, without the Mac, is not usually the same name as MacMahon, though they will concede that Mohan or even Vaughan could, in some cases, be a variation of MacMahon of which the simplified Irish form is now MacMathuna.

O'MALLEY

THE O'Malleys are true Gaels from the West coast and they are celebrated seafarers. The name Malley may have been derived from the old Celtic word for chief—Maglios. They held the chieftainship of two territories in Connacht known now as Burrishoole, and Murrisk in West Mayo. Locally they were called the Manannans, i.e. naval commanders or sea-gods of the Western ocean. Their exploits have been well recorded. It is remarkable that the most famous sea captain should be a woman though the Four Masters who wrote the *Annals* have ignored her existence, as have the Annalists of the *Book of Lough Cè*. Only in Elizabethan State papers is there reliable information about this exceedingly dauntless woman.

She was of course Grania of the O'Malleys of Connacht. She was the daughter of Owen, an O'Malley chieftain, 'strong in galleys and seamen', who carried on a trade in salt fish with Spain and England. Large quantities of salted herrings were exported and there was far more fishing off the southwest coast then than now. English and foreign vessels had to pay a high toll for fishing in Irish waters. Philip II of Spain in 1556 paid £1,000 for leave to fish off the Irish coast for twenty-one years.

Grania O'Malley, sometimes called Granuaile (the bald Grania) because of the legend that she cut her hair short so that she would look like a boy, was reared on the sea and in her long tempestuous life she could never be parted from it.

At about fifteen she was married to Domhnall na Chogagdh (of the battles), the Tanist or heir apparent, of the O'Flahertys of Ballinahinch. These O'Flahertys were the most contentious of all the bellicose clans of Ireland. Grania had three or four children by Domhnall before he was killed in battle.

Grania was well able to look after herself. She raided the territories of the neighbouring chiefs, even to the coast of Scotland. In reply to a question by a British government official who once detained her, Grania said her living was 'maintenance by land and sea', her ruthless method of commerce. She was constantly harried by the cruel Bingham, President of Connacht. One of his men sought hospitality from Grania's son, Owen, and got it generously. Then, calling on his troops he murdered Owen and his men. Such was Connacht in those days.

To strengthen her territory Grania married Richard Burke, another chieftain in Connacht. She stipulated it was only 'for a year certain'. She waited until she'd got his lands, and herself safely installed in his castle and when he returned from a fighting foray she yelled down at him from inside his battlements, 'I dismiss you,' and that was the end of the alliance.

With Richard Burke she had a son, Tibod, who had been born at sea in the middle of an attack by pirates. Grania had to rise from her bed to inspire her men to massacre the pirates. At one stage she went with Tibod to London to get a peerage for him from Queen Elizabeth. She was not successful, but years later, Charles I bestowed on him the title, now extinct, of Viscount Mayo.

Grania fell foul of the powerful FitzGeralds and the Earl of Desmond of that family imprisoned her in Dublin Castle for a while, but relented. She was eventually captured by Sir Richard Bingham who had the gallows all ready for her—

One of Grania O'Malley's Atlantic fortresses, on Clare Island

'For forty years the stay of all rebellions in the West,' he said. But she was rescued by her son-in-law, another Richard Burke.

Between September and December 1588, thousands of men from the Spanish Armada were washed up on the shores of Mayo and Clare and Grania and her henchmen must have been witnesses of this disastrous sea-faring exploit. Eventually, unable herself to return home to her stronghold in Clew Bay because of the loss of all her ships, Grania fled to Ulster, to the O'Neills and the O'Donnells. She corresponded with Queen Elizabeth and is recorded as having visited her in August 1593, when she described herself as a Princess and an equal, though the queen addressed her as Lady Burke. They died about the same time in 1603, Grania in her later years having lived off the pension granted her by the queen.

The O'Malley motto—'*terra marique potens*: powerful both on land and sea', was not always true. When, after the battle of Kinsale in 1601, the old chieftaincies were broken and scattered, the O'Malleys began to go abroad. Life in Ireland became impossible for the Irish and Charles O'Malley and his five brothers all went to France, 'disdaining from the turn affairs then took in that

105

Kingdom to live or serve therein . . . some of whom went up to the frontiers of Hungary to fight against the Turks and were never heard of again. One became a Count of the Empire,' wrote a chronicler of the day. Charles O'Malley who also settled in France comments, 'None of my family was ever known to follow any trade or profession but arms, a cause of not accumulating any considerable fortune since we forfeited our hereditary one.'

This Captain Charles O'Malley, who was at James II's court at St. Germain-en-Laye, wrote to his son in Ireland, Captain Teig O'Malley, late of Colonel Brown's Regiment, telling him how James II had offered him the title of Baron but he had answered, 'I am already Prince as O'Malley, Chief as O'Malley, and the honour his majesty is so graciously pleased to offer could be no addition to me.' He prudently advised Teig, who 'desired the pattents, parchments and titles relevant to our properties in Ireland to be shown to the Court of Claims', that it would be safer to keep them in France, not only because of the uncertainty of the Irish political situation but also because 'some of our lands were added to the estate of the Protestant Archbishop, and the clergy of every persuasion are in general too fond of property to part from what they once get while they can'.

George O'Malley (d. 1843), was a Volunteer in the Castlebar Yeomanry when that town was attacked by the French under Humbert in 1798. In recognition of his services against the rebels he was confirmed as a Lieutenant by Lord Cornwallis. He served with Henry Augustus, 13th Viscount Dillon, who raised the 101st Foot Regiment in which George O'Malley was appointed Major. By his activity and his local connections with County Mayo, he assisted materially in forming the Regiment. He served with it in Ireland and in Jersey and was despatched with three hundred men to St. John's, New Brunswick in 1808, when war with America was imminent. He soldiered in Jamaica, at Quatre Bras, and was at Waterloo where he commanded a battalion of infantry, was twice wounded and had two horses shot under him. When the regiment was disbanded in 1817 his repeated application for employment in Europe was unsuccessful, so he served in the home army.

At the time the French, led by General Humbert, were attacking Castlebar, Austin O'Malley was with the United Irishmen, fighting against the Yeomanry in which George O'Malley was a Volunteer. Austin's son, Patrick, became a general in the army of France. Did these displaced Irishmen know they were opposing their own kinsmen? Was their militancy a matter of principle, or was it purely professional?

From earliest days there were many O'Malley churchmen, including several archbishops of Tuam. The best recorded of them were of a different sept, the O'Malleys of Limerick. Thaddeus O'Malley (1796–1877), born at Garryowen, went to America as a priest but was suspended by his superiors for being 'strong-willed and independent'. From Dublin's pro-cathedral he wrote a series of public letters resolutely demanding a poor law for Ireland and he also supported a system of national education. To demonstrate his view of Irish education he published a *Sketch of the State of Popular Education in Holland, Prussia, Belgium and France*. He also edited a newspaper, *The Social Economist*.

This was much too progressive so he was sent abroad to be Rector of the University at Malta. There he drastically reformed the discipline. Posted back again to Dublin he displeased the church for deprecating the enforced celibacy of clerics.

Thaddeus O'Malley also disagreed with Daniel O'Connell on the question of a complete repeal of the Act of Union. He urged the establishment of a federal parliament for Ireland. This idea was hotly debated and many former disciples of O'Connell flocked to O'Malley's standard. He started another newspaper, *The Federalist*, and tried to unite old and Young Ireland; the former headed by O'Connell favoured moral force while the Young Irelanders advocated arms and deserted O'Connell. After the abortive rising and O'Connell's death, Father Thaddeus O'Malley lived for twenty years in complete retirement in a back lane in Dublin. In 1870 Isaac Butt's new movement for Home Rule found in O'Malley a zealous and energetic ally. Though bold in urging changes in ecclesiastical discipline and advocating social justice, O'Malley was unswerving in his faith; his tragedy was that he was out of his time.

Ernest O'Malley was born in County Mayo in 1898. A medical student at the time of the 1916 rising, he joined the Irish Volunteers. When the Civil War broke out he was a Captain and fought against the Free State soldiers—they were in agreement with the Treaty. He had twenty-one bullets in his body and yet recovered and was able to travel widely to collect funds for the establishment of the *Irish Press*, the paper founded by Eamon De Valera and his party. At various times he was a school teacher in New Mexico and a cab driver in New York. His autobiographical account of the civil war, *On Another Man's Wound*, published in 1936, was an instant classic and was republished in the United States as *Army Without Banners*. He died at Howth, County Dublin, in 1957.

Sir Edward O'Malley, a collateral descendant of Grania, the sea queen, spent nearly all his life abroad as Attorney General or Chief Justice of various colonies, and as Judge of the former extra-territorial court of Egypt and the Ottoman Empire. He died in 1932. His son, Sir Owen St. Clair O'Malley (b.1887) was a diplomat and served in Peking, Mexico, Spain, Hungary, Poland and Portugal. When he retired he wrote his biography, *The Phantom Caravan*, which was published in 1953. He wrote nostalgically of Belclare, and Clew Bay where he had made 'Rockfleet' his home. Lady O'Malley, Ann Bridge, was author of twenty-three books which were best-sellers in the thirties and forties.

The O'Malley name became known in America when Frank Ward O'Malley (1875–1932), born in Pittsburgh, Pennsylvania, began writing for the *Morning Telegraph*. His style was distinguished by 'humorous treatment of trivial happenings', but could change appropriately when reporting dramatic or serious events requiring accurate treatment. In the *American Mercury* in 1929 he dealt with the virtues and weaknesses of the Irish in the United States. His best known book is *The Swiss Family O'Malley*. He also wrote two plays and at the time of his death in France was regarded as one of the best reporters of his generation.

Another recent member of a prominent O'Malley family of Limerick was Donogh O'Malley. A Minister in the Fianna Fail government he shocked the establishment when, as Minister for Education, he set out plans for the unification of Trinity College, Dublin, and University College, Dublin. Before he could attempt to enforce this he died suddenly but his idea still smoulders—without too much fire.

O'Malleys are to be found in the Indian Civil Service, as Colonial Governors and doctors, but not to be found in any reference book is the famous 'Charles O'Malley', the legendary character supposed to typify the devil-may-care Irishman of fiction.

MARTIN (Martyn, MacMartain)

MARTIN, although not distinctively Gaelic, is a quite common name in Ireland as it is in England. The Martins who arrived with the Anglo-Normans became one of the fourteen 'Tribes of Galway'. Robert Martin was Mayor of Galway in 1590. His grandson, Robert, a follower of Charles II, was dispossessed of all his estates in 1654 by Sir Charles Coote, Commander of the Parliamentary troops.

There are various records of native O and Mac Martains. Giolla Earnain O'Martain who died in 1218 was a famous bard and there were several bishops of that name in the fifteenth century.

The sept which went by the name of Mac Giolla Martain has since been anglicized to Gilmartin. Another branch of the original Irish Martins was an off-shoot of the O'Neills in Tyrone. A remarkable aspect of the Martin families, both native and from across the seas, is that not until early in the nineteenth century do they begin to make their mark on Irish history when there was a flowering of politicians, philanthropists and writers.

The Dictionary of National Biography devotes much space to Francis Martin (1652–1722), a member of the Martin tribe of Galway who was driven by the Cromwellian Settlement to seek refuge in Louvain where he became a member of the Augustinian order. It was also a time of great religious turmoil in Europe and Francis Martin joined in the current controversy over the infallibility of the Pope, which he defended. Forseeing the defeats ahead of James II, Francis drew up plans for the assassination of William of Orange, using this as a thesis for his doctorate of theology! Despite protests from the faculty, he won his doctorate from Louvain. His later attack on St. Augustine caused him no setback in his academic and religious progress. He wrote to the Protestant Archbishop of Tuam, suggesting a union between the two faiths which quite impressed the Archbishop. A remarkable priest for his time, he died at Bruges.

Richard Martin (1754–1834) is still remembered in Galway where he lived in feudal splendour in Ballinahinch Castle on an estate of two hundred thousand acres with a drive often described as over thirty miles long. The first of his family to be Protestant, he was educated at Harrow and Cambridge. He was a Colonel of the Galway Volunteers and a friend of George IV, although he had sympathy for Queen Caroline. As High Sheriff for County Galway and a lawyer, it was he who had to condemn to death 'Fighting Fitzgerald' (see George Robert Fitzgerald) with whom he had himself duelled.

Richard Martin is best known as 'Humanity Dick'. His love of animals caused him to take on two British Prime Ministers, Canning and Peel, to win an enactment protecting the rights of animals. He was one of the founders of the Royal Society for the Prevention of Cruelty to Animals. Richard Martin is thought to have been the inspiration for several novels. He is probably the uncle of Charles O'Malley in Lever's novel of that name. Maria Edgeworth's Earl of Glenthorn in *Ennui* is also a Richard Martin type.

Richard (1797–1828) his third son, the first by his second wife, went to Canada where his kinsmen still live. One of his four daughters, Harriet Letitia (1801–

1891) wrote several novels and travelled widely. An account of this Martin family was published privately by Archer E. S. Martin of Winnipeg in 1890.

Thomas Barnewall Martin, Richard's second son, had an only child, Mary Letitia (1815–1858). An ardent philanthropist, she was known as the Princess of Connemara. During the famine, Thomas broke the entail on his vast estates to help with her charities. But he died of the famine fever. There was no money to pay the mortgages and Mary Letitia lost her inheritance. Now penniless, she went to Belgium where she began writing. She was known as Letitia Bell Martin—her husband Arthur Bell had combined his name with hers. In an attempt to try their fortune in the New World they sailed for America, but she died in childbirth shortly after landing. *Julia Howard*, published in 1850, is an autobiographical account of the famine in Connemara.

Sir Samuel Martin (1801–1883) was of the Ulster Martins. Born in Culmore, County Derry, he graduated in Law from Trinity College, Dublin, and practised in London. He was a judge for nearly a quarter of a century.

Robert Montgomery Martin (1803–1868) was also from Ulster. He came from County Tyrone and when still in his teens went to Ceylon. This was the beginning of a series of world travels which laid the basis for his *History of the British Colonies* which obtained for him an introduction to George IV. He used his pen zealously for the improvement of British colonialism, not least in his native country. In 1845, while in Hong Kong, he disagreed with the Governor over raising revenue from the sale of opium and resigned his office. He wrote prodigiously on a global scale, on handloom weaving in Ireland, the antiquities of Eastern India, the monetary system of British India, steam navigation in Australia, the Hudson's Bay Territories and Vancouver Island. He died, aged sixty-five, in England.

John Martin (1812–1875) was born at Loughorne, County Down. While studying at Trinity College, Dublin, he became involved in the politics of the Repeal Association. His brother-in-law was the patriot John Mitchel and when Mitchel was deported to Tasmania, John Martin published a revolutionary paper, *The Irish Felon*, which caused him to be transported for ten years to Van Diemen's Land. In 1854, when he returned to Ireland, he established the National League and was a Member of Parliament for County Meath. He was known everywhere as 'Honest John Martin'.

Sir James Martin (1815–1886) was born in Fermoy, County Cork. He was a small child when his family emigrated to Australia. In Sydney where he was both journalist and solicitor, he rose to become Attorney General. He was three times Premier of Australia.

Violet Martin (1862–1915) of Galway, was the Ross half of that immortal cousinly duo, Somerville and Ross, who wrote the now classic *Experiences of an Irish R.M.*, *The Real Charlotte*, etc. Ross came from the ancient family seat outside Galway. Although Violet died long before her partner, the books still continued to flow from Miss Somerville's pen as though Miss Martin were still with her—as indeed she seems to have believed she was, at least in the spirit.

Edward Martyn (1859–1923) of Masonbrook, County Galway, was educated in Dublin and Oxford. He founded the Feis Ceoil, the annual Irish musical festival held in Dublin. With W. B. Yeats and Lady Gregory he founded the Irish Literary Theatre—now the famous Abbey Theatre.

He wrote a number of plays, took an active part in the language revival and in

Edward Martyn, politician and outstanding influence in Irish culture (1859–1923)

the improvement of church music. His celebrated sparring with his fellow writer and Galway colleague, George Moore, was spiked with wit and malice. He was President and co-founder of Sinn Fein, the Irish nationalist party which campaigned for Home Rule. Edward Martyn, despite his many eccentricities, did more to vitalize Irish culture than has yet been acknowledged.

With a non-committal name such as Martin, it is difficult to separate the Irish Martins from the many others. There are descendants of Irish Martins in Canada, Australia, America. Henry Newall Martin (1848–1896), born in Newry, County Down, one of the dozen children of a Congregational Minister, was taken to America at a tender age. His brilliant mind overcame a minimal education and from Medical School at London University he won a scholarship to Cambridge. He was the first to hold the chair of biology in the newly founded Johns Hopkins University in Baltimore, where he was described as having put 'physiology in its proper relation to the science and art of medicine'.

110

MOORE (O'More)

I T would be impossible today to differentiate exactly between the ancient Gaelic Moores and the Moores who came to Ireland seven hundred years ago. It is a quite common name also in Britain. Ó Mórdha is the Irish spelling which comes from Mordha, majestic. They were chieftains of Leix, and Abbeyleix gets its name from the Cistercian Abbey founded there in 1183 by Conor O'More. On the estate belonging to Lord and Lady de Vesci there is a tomb with a carved effigy of Malachi O'More, said to be the last of their chieftains. Six miles from Abbeyleix a garage marks the Pass of the Plumes, so called because it was here the O'Moores, in 1599, are said to have killed five hundred of the Earl of Essex's men whose plumed helmets were strewn all around.

High up on the Rock of Dunamase a few miles outside Portlaoise in County Leix, the magnificent ruins of a stronghold of the O'Mores are outlined against the sky. It must have made a superb setting for the inauguration of their chieftains. Here, too, Owen Roe O'Neill made his headquarters during the Cromwellian invasion.

Rory is probably the greatest O'More. He was the leader of the old Irish who fought valiantly against the Tudors. His son, Owney MacRory O'More, got back some of his inheritance. He once held prisoner James Butler, Duke of Ormonde, general of the Irish royalist army and Lord Lieutenant, and released him with a millstone around his neck! It was in a skirmish with the O'Mores that Garret

The capture of Ormonde by O'Moore

Mor, Gerald Fitzgerald, the uncrowned king of Ireland, was killed. Patrick Sarsfield, one of Ireland's greatest soldiers, had an O'More mother.

The Viscounts of Drogheda, whose family name is Moore, descend from a soldier who came from Kent. Mellifont, County Louth, was their home and one of them, Sir Garrett Moore, became so good a friend of Hugh O'Neill, Earl of Tyrone, a former foe, that in 1607, before his flight to Spain, O'Neill stayed with him, weeping bitterly when taking his leave, but saying nothing of his tragic departure. The descendants of these Moores later moved to Moore Abbey, County Kildare, afterwards the home of Count John MacCormack and now a convent.

In three-and-a-half centuries there has been but one Catholic Provost of Trinity College, Dublin. He was the Reverend Michael Moore (1640–1726) who was appointed by James II. With the librarian, McCarthy, he saved Trinity library from being burned. A most able man, he was banished because of an indiscretion. Preaching before James II he unfortunately took the text, 'If the blind lead the blind both shall fall into the ditch.' James' Jesuit confessor who had poor eyesight took this personally. Moore was dismissed and went abroad, to Rome and later to France where he was Rector of the University of Paris. The fine library he bequeathed to the Irish College which he had established there had almost disappeared at his death, stolen by a servant who took advantage of the blindness which ironically afflicted Moore in his later years.

Arthur Moore was one of the earliest economists (1666–1730). Born in Monaghan, he made his money and his home in England. An advocate of free trade, he promoted the Treaty of Commerce with France and Spain in 1712.

Henry Moore (1751–1844) born in Dublin went to London to work as a woodcarver and became the devoted servant of John Wesley who appointed him one of his literary executors. He wrote a life of Wesley and despite many chances of improvement he kept to the austere life of a travelling preacher.

It was Thomas Moore (1779–1852) who brought greatest fame to the name. The son of a Dublin grocer, he managed to get into Trinity College, Dublin, when in 1793 it was opened to Catholics. Here he met all the leading revolutionaries but was restrained by his mother from actively joining them. He quickly made a name, but no money, as a poet in London. Patrons secured him a government appointment in Bermuda. He endured it for four months before finding a deputy while he toured America and Canada. Returning to London, he fell in love, married and wrote love poems for his wife. He dared to satirize the Prince of Wales. *Lalla Rookh*, his oriental poem, was a great success. Meanwhile, in Bermuda his deputy absconded leaving him a debt of £6,000 which forced Moore to travel abroad to escape his creditors. In Italy he met Lord Byron who gave him his autobiography which was not to be published till after his death. Byron died almost immediately after making this gift and Moore sold the book, but was persuaded by the Byron family to withdraw it. He gave back the money, but alas burned the book! Later he wrote his own life of Byron.

Although he was popular in Ireland for *Moore's Melodies*, his nostalgic songs of Erin, he would not take part in politics, despite Daniel O'Connell's persuasion. His statue stands on a traffic island close to Trinity College, Dublin.

George Henry Moore (1810–1870) of Moore Hall, County Mayo, was a wealthy landowner whose family, like a number of other Irish families of that era, had made their money in Europe in the wine business. At the time of the tenant right movement George Henry Moore was a compelling speaker and an

The poet Thomas Moore (1779–1852)

M.P. for Mayo. He believed in Home Rule and was a colleague of Charles Gavan Duffy. His wife was a grand-daughter of John Browne, 1st Earl of Altamont of Westport House (q.v.).

George Augustus Moore (1852–1933) was their eldest son. He was educated in England and France. His father died when he was eighteen and he was torn between managing his Irish estates and writing in London. His first novels shocked the Victorian public, while at the same time establishing him as a serious writer. *Esther Waters* written in 1894 is probably the book by which he will be best remembered. It has been filmed. He returned to Ireland to help in the founding of the Abbey Theatre in Dublin. He was not an easy man to get on with and quarrels interspersed with cutting *bon mots* seemed to pursue him. He died at his home, in Ebury Street, Chelsea.

Robert Ross Rowan Moore (1811–1864) born in Dublin, was the eldest son of William Moore of an Ulster family. He was a political economist and a close friend of the patriot Thomas Davis. A member of the Irish anti-slavery society, in 1841, at Limerick, he put a stop to a scheme for the exportation of apprentices to the West Indies. He campaigned for free trade.

His only son, Norman (1847–1922) was dean of St. Bartholomew's Hospital, London, and an Irish scholar.

Temple Lushington Moore (1856–1920) who came from Tullamore in Offaly, was an important British architect, concentrating on church architecture.

Brian Moore, born in Belfast in 1921, after the 1939–1945 war went to Canada. There he wrote a best-seller, *Judith Hearne*, which has been followed by *The Feast of Lupercal*, *The Luck of Ginger Coffey* (made into a film), and various other successful novels.

113

MURPHY (O'Murchadha, O'Morchoe)

THE Murphy name is the most numerous in all Ireland, and the most scattered. There have been notable Murphy families in every province with the possible exception of Connacht. In Cork, Wexford, Carlow, Armagh they have predominated. Murphys figured largely in the lists of the Irish Brigades on the Continent; they contributed to the expansion of Australia, and in the United States they have dominated the police and the law, and played active roles in politics, commerce and the arts.

In his book *Irish Names and Surnames*, Father Patrick Woulfe suggests that Murphy means sea-warrior. One sept was of the Cinel Eoghain who were chiefs

Arthur Murphy (1727–1805), actor and author

of Siol Aodha in the present County Tyrone. A second family originated from the Ul Fiachrach who were chiefs around Sligo Bay, but they were driven away by the Anglo-Norman invasions. Another branch who were chiefs of Ui Feilme were prominent in County Wexford.

In most Irish families a definite thread prevails. In the Murphys, perhaps because they were apparently neither close-knit nor warlike, there is a whole skein of threads to be unravelled.

There were the writers. Firstly, John Murphy—Seán Ó Murchadha na Raithíneach—the name of the village in Cork where he was born in 1700 and died about seventy years later, was the last recognized head of the Blarney bards.

Arthur Murphy (1727–1805) was born into a distinguished family at Clonquin, Roscommon. He typifies the versatility that flows through the Murphy histories. He gained fame as both actor and author. As became the custom, he was educated in France and afterwards joined his mother in London. Refusing to go into business with his wealthy relatives, he joined London literary circles and began to write for the periodicals. Eventually, lack of expected family finance drove him to the stage where he appeared at Drury Lane, directed by Garrick. He wrote plays and, despite an embargo on actors at that time, managed to get into Lincoln's Inn to study law. At sixty-one he retired from the theatre and the bar, enriched by his labours and by an inheritance from the West Indies. But he got into debt, attempting to publish translations of Tacitus and Sallust and other literary works.

His elder brother, James (1725–1759), adopted his mother's name, French, and, as James Murphy French, also took part in the legal and literary life of London.

John Joseph Murphy (1827–1894), was born in Belfast of Quaker parentage. He was a mill owner yet managed to publish volumes of verse and works on science and religion.

Denis Murphy (1833–1896) was born in County Cork and educated in England, Germany and Spain. He became a Jesuit priest and a Professor of History and Literature at University College, Dublin. He published historical writings and was a vice president of the Royal Irish Academy.

There are artists in the Murphy family too. John Murphy (1740–1820) left his native Cork to study engraving in London where he was regarded as a master of the mezzotint, making plates for the nobility and the family of George III.

Denis Brownell Murphy had to leave Dublin in 1798 because of his political

Seamus Murphy, a leading Irish sculptor, with busts of Michael Collins, Sean Lemass and Archbishop McQuaid

115

allegiance to the United Irishmen. In London he made his name as a miniaturist, becoming at one time painter to the Princess Charlotte. What fame he had achieved was surpassed by his daughter, Anna Brownell Jameson, who wrote with great knowledge on art.

Sculpture has been successfully followed by three men of Cork. Thomas J. Murphy, born in 1881, the son of John Murphy, also a sculptor, went to London where he executed many public commissions. Seamus Murphy, born in County Cork in 1910, is one of Ireland's leading sculptors. His book *Stone Mad*, published in 1950, has been reprinted.

The Murphys have had their share of bishops. In the eighteenth century Edward Murphy was archbishop of Dublin. Francis Murphy (1795–1858), born at Navan, County Meath, went to Australia and became bishop of Adelaide.

John Murphy (1772–1847), Bishop of Cork, was a scholar who amassed the largest private library in Ireland, most of which was sold in London with the exception of the Irish manuscripts which were bequeathed to Maynooth College, County Kildare.

Canon Jeremiah Murphy (1840–1915) of Cork, was also an Irish scholar who collected rare books. His library weighed fifteen tons when it came under the hammer in Cork after his death.

The annalists record many distinguished Murphy scholars. James Gracey (1808–1896) of County Down, a Presbyterian Minister, wrote Latin and Hebrew grammars and many biblical and philosophical works.

Francis Stack (1807–1860), a brother of John Murphy, Bishop of Cork, was a clever lawyer, an M.P. for Cork and a scholar who assisted Francis Sylvester Mahony, the famous humorist 'Father Prout', by his contributions to his *Reliques*.

His first cousin, Jeremiah Daniel Murphy (1806–1824), was a boy genius who mastered seven languages, wrote verse in various languages, contributed to intellectual magazines but died very young.

James Cavanagh Murphy, whose parental origins are obscure, was born near Cork (1750–1814). Beginning his working life as a bricklayer, followed by study in a Dublin art school and years abroad in Spain, he became one of the century's leading authorities on Moorish architecture. He was also one of the architects consulted about alterations to London's House of Commons and assisted with its extensions. He was an antiquarian and published many works and drawings on his subject, which are preserved in numerous museums and libraries.

Robert Murphy (1806–1843), a man quite out of his time and place, was one of the numerous children of a shoemaker of Mallow, County Cork. An accident to his leg at the age of eleven caused him to be confined to bed for a year. This drove him to reading Euclid, and developed in him such remarkable mathematical proficiency that he was encouraged by a local teacher. Friends assisted his transfer to Cambridge where he eventually was ordained in the Church of England and elected a fellow. His social habits were not on a par with his scholarship and he had to leave Cambridge to seek a living teaching and writing in London. He died at thirty-seven, leaving a vast number of mathematical memoirs.

Possibly the two most revered Murphys in Ireland are the patriot priests, Father John and Father Michael Murphy who were both killed in the bloody revolt centred around Wexford in 1798. Many ballads have been written about Father John Murphy of Boulavogue.

Marie-Louise Murphy, painted by Boucher

The outstanding woman of the Murphys was undoubtedly Marie Louise Murphy (1737–1814), the fifth daughter of an Irish soldier who had settled at Rouen as a shoemaker. After his death her mother took the family to Paris where they found jobs as actresses and models. Marie Louise posed for Boucher which brought her to the notice of Louis XV, who made her his mistress. Their child is supposed to have been General de Beaufranchet. She was married three times and divorced by her third husband who was thirty years younger than she. During the Reign of Terror she suffered imprisonment.

Patrick Murphy achieved notoriety of a rare variety. Born in County Down in 1834, he grew to be the tallest man in Europe—eight feet and one inch. He exhibited himself everywhere except Ireland but when he died, aged twenty-eight, his embalmed remains came back to County Down.

Another Patrick Murphy achieved short-lived notoriety as a weather prophet who published a weather almanack. By sheer chance he predicted that the 20th January of 1838 would be the coldest day of winter and when it was, he became a celebrity. He was never able to repeat that first stroke of luck.

William Martin Murphy (1844–1921) of Bantry, County Cork, was one of the first modern Irish business tycoons. He inaugurated railways and tramways in Ireland, Britain and Africa. He owned stores and the *Irish Independent* newspaper and was an M.P. He refused the knighthood offered him by Edward VII

117

during his visit to Ireland in 1907. In the 1913 general strike in Dublin he earned the obloquy of the workers by his opposition to their cause.

It is difficult to do justice to the Murphys who went abroad. They are well represented in Australia, especially in the legal and medical sphere. Francis Murphy (1809–1891) of Cork went to Sydney as a colonial surgeon. He settled there and went into farming and politics and was knighted in 1860. He died in Melbourne.

North and South, the Murphys have sought their fortunes and given their services to the whole continent of America. In the United States there are probably now more Murphys than in Ireland. Henry Cruse Murphy (1810–1882), was the grandson of an Irish doctor who had emigrated to the New World. He practised law in Brooklyn and was its mayor for many years. He served in the state Senate and, besides being a most forward-thinking promoter of local developments like railways and Brooklyn Bridge, he was also a scholar who amassed a fine library.

John Murphy (1812–1880) of Omagh, Tyrone, was brought to the United States as a child. He, too, had that remarkable feeling for books, typical of so many of the Murphys. He was a book publisher. Murphy and Company specialized in theological, particularly Catholic, books from his headquarters in Baltimore.

John Benjamin Murphy (1857–1916) was of Irish parentage. He became one of the leading professors of Surgery in Chicago, and invented the famous Murphy button which simplified the technique of abdominal operations.

The progress of temperance reform was greatly advanced by Francis Murphy (1836–1907) of County Wexford who arrived penniless in New York at the age of sixteen. He led a dissipated life for many years until a term in prison brought him in contact with a reformer which led to him taking a pledge of total abstinence. He developed into a dynamic preacher in the cause of temperance, drawing thousands to his meetings and, it is said, causing the closure of five hundred saloons in Allegheny and the adjoining counties. He carried his reform campaign through to Canada and Australia and other countries.

Tammany Hall, the New York headquarters of the Democratic Party, reached its peak under the leadership of Charles Francis Murphy (1858–1924), the son of poor Irish immigrants who spent his childhood in East Side, New York. A manager of men, he worked his way up from the dockyards to become a successful politician and a master of strategic diplomacy. Shrewd in the world of business, he made his money from real estate and was held in esteem because of his remarkable aloofness from the various corrupting influences against which he quietly worked.

Frank Murphy's grandfather was hanged by the British. His father emigrated to the U.S.A. and was jailed for his part in the Fenian attack on Canada. In 1933 Frank Murphy, who had studied law in Dublin and London, was Governor General of the Philippines, was Governor of his native Michigan in 1936, and was U.S. Attorney General in 1939. He died in 1949.

Ireland has contributed greatly to the policing of New York. Two of its most able Police Commissioners have been Murphys. Thomas Murphy, a Police Commissioner of New York City in 1951 was afterwards a Federal Judge and the prosecutor at the Hiss trials. Michael J. Murphy, also a New York City Police Commissioner, led the drive against corruption in the nineteen-sixties.

MACNAMARA

THE name of MacNamara has always been associated with County Clare, the rugged West coast where the Atlantic pounds the fearsome Cliffs of Moher. Their name is from the sea—MacConmara—son of Cu-mara, hound of the sea. Next to the O'Briens they were the most powerful of the Dalcassian clans who are said to descend from Caisin, son of Cas who was the common ancestor of all the Dál gCais, one of the most ancient peoples of Ireland. As hereditary marshals of Thomond it was the MacNamaras' privilege to inaugurate the chief of the O'Briens who was very often also a king. They were lords of Clancullen—the greater part of East Clare. Eventually they divided into two septs, the chief of the West Clancullen being described as MacNamara Fyne (fiionn, fair), and the chief of East Clancullen was MacNamara Reagh (riabhach, swarthy or grizzled).

They were well chronicled by the Four Masters between 1099 and 1600, and the records feature the names of their West Clancullen strongholds; Moyrish, Creevagh, Cratleagh, Ballynacreige, Ballynasliebh, Muckane and Rathffelane. There seems little enough account of their deeds on sea during that period, but on land there is a wealth of evidence that they were insatiable builders. It is recorded that the MacNamaras built forty-two castles. In 1402 they founded the Franciscan Abbey of Quin, which, though greatly ruined, remains a place rich in atmosphere. In 1467 Sean MacNamara, Lord of Clancullen, built Knappogue Castle and finished the building of Bunratty Castle which his father, Sioda, had begun in 1433.

The fortifications built by the MacNamaras and the O'Briens, mostly to protect themselves from neighbouring attack, were no protection against Cromwell's technically superior forces. After 1650 there is a long gap in the records of the MacNamaras of Clare.

Their castles at Knappogue and Bunratty have had exceedingly chequered careers and have passed through many hands, though today, unlike Quin Abbey, they have been restored. They are part of the string of Clare castles acquired by the Shannon Free Airport Development Company who, seeing their tourist potential, were inspired to revitalize them. Bunratty Castle, surrounded by its splendid folk park, is the setting for medieval banquets. Knappogue, built fifty years before Columbus discovered America, is now the property of an American family who continue to enrich it and encourage the medieval banquets which are held there during the summer months when it is enlivened by music, poetry and dancing for the entertainment of international visitors.

Although the Cromwellians dispersed the MacNamaras, they did not annihilate them. Many went to France and it was in the navy, rather than the army, their name was prominent. One of the most famous of the MacNamaras who went abroad is Count MacNamara who, in the first year of the Revolution, was Commodore of the French Fleet in the Far East where he had played a useful role as a diplomatist. In September 1790 he put into the Indian port of Ile de France, but the colonists and soldiers of the French garrison there, who had heard of his hostility to the principles of the Revolution, assassinated him.

Captain Francis MacNamara, Captain in the 8th Hussars, a distinguished soldier and M.P. for Clare

James MacNamara (1768–1826) from Clare, was in the British navy where he saw much service up to the Peace of Amiens. In a duel, following a fight between two dogs, he killed his opponent and in 1803 was tried for murder. Nelson, Hood and others almost as distinguished, testified to his character and service as a very popular officer and he was acquitted. In 1814 he became Admiral James MacNamara.

Genealogical papers relating to the MacNamara family are widespread. Some are in the Bibliothèque Nationale, Paris, and in the British Museum there is a letter in French from Queen Mary II to the Abbess of Ronchery at Angers, thanking her for helping Miss MacNamara whose father served as a Major in the King's Troop.

'Fireball' MacNamara brought no lustre to the name as he shot his way through France, like an early cowboy. Back in his native Clare he continued his aggressive ways, robbing and killing, and ending on the scaffold. He is buried in the Abbey of Quin built by his ancestor, beside a gentleman who died in a quarrel with him.

Donnchada Ruadh MacConmara, who was born c.1709, in East Clare, was educated in Rome for the priesthood. His character was not in accord with its discipline and he was expelled, then finding his vocation was poetry. He was at the Court of Poetry held by Piaras MacGearailt in Cork in 1743. He earned his living for a while as a schoolmaster in Waterford from which there was much traffic to and from Newfoundland. It seems Donnchada Ruadh made the voyage for he wrote a poem, *The Adventures of a Luckless Fellow*, describing the very hazardous voyage made by an emigrant.

If he did get to Newfoundland he must have returned for he again taught in a school in Ireland, being dismissed for drunkenness. He turned from Protestant to Catholic and back again to qualify for various jobs. He also travelled in Europe, which may have given him the inspiration for that lovely poem full of nostalgia, *Bán Chnoic Éireann Óigh* (*The Fair Hills of Ireland*), which sounds infinitely better in Irish. His *Song of Repentance*, written towards the close of his days, is considered to be far above the sentimental literature of other writers of the eighteenth century.

120

O'NEILL

THE O'Briens, O'Connors and O'Neills are among the leading Gaelic families of Ireland. The Great O'Neill line can be traced back to the thirteenth century. These O'Neills—the name means 'champion'—have inspired many poets, writers and musicians. From the eleventh to the seventeenth century the O'Neills of Ulster dominate Irish history. They were High Kings of Ireland and claim descent from King Conn of the Hundred Battles and from King Niall of the Nine Hostages whose raids into Britain are supposed to have captured Saint Patrick for Ireland around A.D. 405.

Domhnall, born about A.D. 943, was the first of the family to use the O'Neill surname, a name which survives today most numerously and in several different versions, including Norse, and ranging from Nihill to Nielson or even Nelson.

There are four distinct families located in various parts of Ireland. O'Neill is one of the few Gaelic names which has the same spelling in English as in Irish.

The sept who were most prominent in the Middle Ages were the Ulster O'Neills. They divided into great families with minor branches. These are the Clandeboy O'Neills of Antrim and Down, and the Tyrone O'Neills.

The Clandeboy branch was named after Hugh, the Fair-haired, in Irish, Aodh Buidhe. He was the twenty-seventh in descent from King Nial of the Nine Hostages and he won back large areas of Antrim and Down for his Clann Aodha Bhuidhe, anglicized Clandeboy. Cromwell's wars finally scattered the Clandeboy O'Neills. Direct descendants of that Royal House have long been settled in Portugal where the family of Dom Hugh O'Neill live at Lisbon.

Shane's Castle, stronghold of the O'Neills

Shane's Castle in County Down, where the last of the Clandeboys of the Gaelic order lived, is today occupied by Lord O'Neill of the Maine who, as Captain Terence O'Neill, was Prime Minister of Northern Ireland from 1963 to 1969. He inherited through the female line from an ancestor, the Reverend Arthur Chichester who assumed the illustrious name of O'Neill.

The O'Neills of Tyrone tried by every warlike means available to keep out the medieval colonizers. Undoubtedly they also frittered a great deal of time and

energy in dynastic battling. In fact, they were overthrown by the great Brian Boru (q.v.) just before he won the Battle of Clontarf in 1014.

The proud Shane O'Neill (1530–1567), the greatest O'Neill of the old Gaelic order, would sign himself 'Misi O'Neill', signifying his chieftaincy.

Hugh, the Great O'Neill (1540–1616), was at one time Baron of Dungannon and Earl of Tyrone. Queen Elizabeth had him at her court for six years, hoping to convert him into a Queen's man. Returning home to Ulster he failed to support her, yet was powerless against her country's superior strength. Eventually she forced him into giving up his Gaelic title—The O'Neill—the magical title of a chosen Irish chieftain without which his people would not trust him.

When the Spaniards landed at Kinsale, Hugh O'Neill had joined with Red Hugh O'Donnell to make the three hundred miles march south to join battle

122

with them against the English. In the decisive battle at Kinsale in 1601 they were defeated utterly and, eventually, Hugh O'Neill joined O'Donnell in exile abroad. To their tombs in the Spanish National Church beside the Villa Spada, the Irish Embassy to the Holy See in Rome, come many Irish pilgrims.

Between the Tyrone O'Neills and Spain there had long been close contact. Philip II had made great efforts to help them. General Owen Roe (the red-haired) (1590–1649) served in the Spanish army for thirty years and returned at last to serve his own country. Just as he was gaining power he died.

Hugh MacArt, who returned from Spain with Owen Roe, was a Major General of the Ulster Irish. He repulsed Oliver Cromwell at Clonmel but had to surrender Limerick to Ireton in 1651. He returned to Spain where he died in 1660.

Daniel, a nephew of Owen Roe, strangely nicknamed 'Infallible Subtle', was born in 1612 and was a Protestant Cavalier who had great influence with Charles II of England who made him his Postmaster General. In a later generation the very same office was bestowed on Charles Henry St. John, first and last Earl O'Neill (1779–1841), of Shane's Castle, who was also Grand Master of the Orangemen.

The O'Neills of Ulster were a fiercely proud, sometimes arrogant, clan. Although their royal dynasty has long since faded, their fame still lives in many parts of the world, particularly in Europe where O'Neills fought valiantly in the armies of Spain, France, Austria, the Netherlands. There were also distinguished O'Neills in the church and the arts. The Red Hand of Ulster, the device on their coat of arms, is the symbol of that troubled northern province until this day.

The wandering blind harper Arthur (1737–1816) is recorded as having said, 'Wherever an O'Neill sits is always the head of the table'. This Arthur O'Neill was the root stock from which has sprung some of the best in Irish traditional music.

In the eighteenth century, long after the great dynasty had faded, came the new order with John O'Neill who supported Catholic Emancipation. He was also one of the delegates who, in 1789, went from the Irish Parliament to request George, Prince of Wales, to assume the regency. In 1798, defending Antrim against the rebels, John was wounded and died.

Another John (1777–c.1860), a shoemaker of Munster, went to London where he wrote a novel, *Mary of Avonmore*, and also much temperance poetry. His play, *The Drunkard*, was illustrated by Cruikshank.

Eliza O'Neill, born in Drogheda, County Louth, in 1791, the daughter of a theatre manager, went on the stage and became first, the rave of Dublin, then of London and Paris.

Henry O'Neill, born in Dundalk, in 1800, was an archaeologist and lithographer.

Hugh O'Neill, born in 1784, was the son of an Irish architect who designed a portion of Portland Place, London. He was noted for his fine architectural drawings, some of which are in the British Museum.

Joseph O'Neill (1886–1953), an Irish Civil Servant with the Department of Education, was a best-selling novelist who won the Harmsworth Award for *Wind from the North*.

In America, James O'Neill (1849–1920) had played Edmond Danton in the

Arthur O'Neill (1737–1816), the blind harper who had a lasting influence on Irish traditional music

Count of Monte Cristo six thousand times when he died. He had emigrated from Kilkenny at the age of five to join his family and he became one of America's leading actors.

He was the father of the great American dramatist, Eugene O'Neill (1888–1953), who was born in New York and, having worked as actor, gold prospector, seaman and at a variety of other jobs, began to write plays when he was confined to hospital with tuberculosis. In 1936 he was awarded the Nobel prize.

'Sweet Peggy O'Neill' (1769–1879) almost sundered the United States of America. Daughter of a Washington tavern keeper of Hibernian origins, she had beauty, wit and vivacity. She married secondly, John Henry Eaton, a Tennessee politician, a member of the U.S. Senate and a close personal friend of President Jackson. In 1829 he appointed John Henry Eaton Secretary of War. This sudden elevation of Peggy O'Neill was bitterly resented by the other wives, so much so that Jackson reorganized his cabinet with the result that Martin Van Buren, Secretary of State who took Jackson's side, became first Vice-President, then President. Eaton was U.S. Minister in Spain in 1836–1840. After his death, Peggy married again, and divorced.

John O'Neill (1834–1878) from County Monaghan took his nationalism with him when he went to America. First he served in the army there with great success. Then he was with the Fenian Brotherhood who attacked Canada from Buffalo in 1866 with the peculiar idea of invading Canada in the cause of Irish freedom. He survived to become a civilian working for a firm of land speculators and the chief town of Holt County bears his name.

NUGENT (de Nuinnseann)

HUGH de Nugent with his cousins, Gilbert and Richard, came to Ireland with William the Conqueror and, we are told, could trace their ancestry back eleven generations to Albert, Comte de Perche of Normandy, A.D. 930. In Ireland, where they were given generous grants of land, the Nugents were to become variously Barons Delvin and Lords Westmeath, Westmeath being the county in which they mostly settled.

Nugents in every walk of life are numerous all over Ireland, as indeed they are in England. In very early days some of the already anglicized Nugents crossed to Ireland to settle in Cork where they formed a clan in the Irish fashion, based on Aghavarten Castle, near Carrigaline.

The Nugents of Ballinlough Castle, County Westmeath, through marriage, were allied to the O'Reillys, Lords of Breffney. The Nugents who married Grevilles joined their names to retain the Nugent patrimony. There is a Greville-Nugent family mausoleum at Fore, that ancient place where St. Fechin had his well. The church was rebuilt by one of the Nugents.

Not far off is Delvin, a pretty village from which the Nugents took their title and where they built a castle. From Delvin they afterwards moved to nearby Clonyn Castle.

The Nugents, as did most of the Normans, identified themselves with the ancient Irish. There is an account of Andrew Nugent of Donore who, in 1641, was a captain in the Irish army which defended Kilsoglin against the English. For this both he and his son were indicted. In the wake of the disasters which followed the 1641 rising many of the Nugents left Ireland and there are records of them in the archives of Austria, Belgium, France, Spain and Italy. In fact, manuscripts relating to them are remarkably plentiful. In 1622 Francis Nugent, a Capuchin friar wrote to Rome complaining of the book written by Philip O'Sullivan. In the Stuart Mss. there is a warrant of 1704 in which James III admits Ann Nugent to be a Bedchamber Woman to his sister, the Princess. In Paris archives there is mention of allowances being made to the women of the Irish regiments to rejoin their husbands in Italy where they were probably serving in Nugents' Regiment of Horse.

There are many former Nugent castles all over Westmeath. Although they are mostly in ruins, or in other hands, accounts of the families who built them occupy no less than eighteen pages in *The Dictionary of National Biography*, a British publication in which Irish biographies earn a remarkable amount of space.

Sir Richard Nugent, the 10th Baron Delvin, who inherited through his mother, was an enthusiastic devastator of the Irish, for which he was financially and otherwise rewarded. He was Lord-Deputy of Ireland under the Earl of Ormonde. He died about 1475.

Another Sir Richard, the 12th Baron, was also very loyal to the English Crown. He sided with Gerald, 8th Earl of Kildare against Clanricarde and the Irish chiefs. He replaced Kildare and, as Lord Deputy, governed for a while. In a dispute with Brian O'Conor over a pension that Delvin withheld, O'Conor took him hostage, only releasing him after much bloodshed and on payment of the pension. In his zeal to protect the English Pale, Delvin pursued Brian O'Conor to Offaly where in 1538 he razed Brian's castle at Dangan but was himself killed.

Richard Nugent (1583–1642), 15th Baron Delvin and 1st Earl of Westmeath, had a chequered career. Thinking himself unjustly deprived of land on which he had spent a fortune, he joined the anti-government conspiracy of 1606. It misfired and he was imprisoned in Dublin Castle, from which he escaped and was on the run for two years. Eventually he won back King James' favour. In 1641, his refusal to join with the Irish gentry in the rising against the English led to his intimidation and assassination.

His grandson, Richard (d.1684), 2nd Earl of Westmeath, was whole-heartedly a Jacobite, yet in 1652 he submitted to Cromwell's Parliament. After many vicissitudes he had most of his estates returned to him at the Restoration. It was he who rebuilt the chapel at Fore where he and many of his descendants are buried.

John, 5th Earl of Westmeath (1672–1754), was a professional soldier who fought in practically every battle in Europe during his lifetime. He married an Italian Countess and their son, Thomas, the 6th Earl, was the first of the Westmeath line to conform to the Protestant established religion.

Christopher is another name that runs through the Nugent family. Sir Christopher (1544–1602), the 14th Baron Delvin, was educated at Cambridge under the eye of Queen Elizabeth. Nonetheless, he spent his life being suspected of treasons, and ended it in Dublin Castle. He left behind *A primer of the Irish Language, compiled at the request and for the use of Queen Elizabeth*. He appears to have been a man of moderate views living in extreme times.

Christopher Nugent (d.1751) of Dardistown, County Meath, after the siege of Limerick, elected to take his sword abroad. He changed the name of the Regiment of Sheldon to that of Nugent but was deprived of his regiment for following the Old Pretender to Scotland.

An advance in the cure of hydrophobia was made by Christopher Nugent (d.1775) of Meath, who studied medicine in France and practised it in Bath. Edmund Burke was married to his daughter. When Christopher moved to London he became a popular member of the famous Literary Club favoured by Boswell.

Thomas was the first name of three prominent Nugents. Thomas, 4th Earl of Westmeath (1656–1752) served with King James' army at the Boyne and at the siege of Limerick. After much intervening dissension over land and allegiances, he died half a century later, aged ninety-six.

Thomas Nugent (1715), a second son of the 2nd Earl of Westmeath, was Baron of Riverston and Chief Justice of Ireland. He was considered to be over-zealous in reversing the outlawries enacted against his Catholic countrymen and he revived an ancient act to deprive the Protestants of their guns. In his political adherence he fell between two stools, was regarded as a traitor by the Irish rebels and was himself outlawed by the English after the siege of Limerick, but he was allowed to retain his lands.

The army, the law and politics were the careers followed by many of the Nugents. Thomas Nugent (1710–1772) was an exception. Meath born and a graduate of Trinity College, Dublin, he was a scholar who wrote widely on history, linguistics, travel and French literature. He made his home in London.

Christopher Nugent (d.1742), an Irish gentleman who entered the service of the Republic of Venice and attained the rank of general

The word to 'nugentize' grew from the activities of Robert Nugent of Carlanstown, County Westmeath (1702–1788). A politician and a poet he trimmed his sails to suit every wind. He amassed a fortune by marrying a trio of ladies, all well-endowed by previous husbands. They were described as being 'nugentized' by his acquaintances who included Johnson, Walpole, Goldsmith and the Prince of Wales. The Prince borrowed money from Nugent, and was not able to repay him. After the Prince's death he was recompensed by George III who created him Viscount Clare and Baron Nugent in 1766.

George Nugent (1757–1849), a natural son of a Westmeath Nugent, died aged ninety-two, in his Berkshire manor, a baronet and a retired Field-Marshal. A product of the Royal Military Academy, Woolwich, he served with many British regiments and was in America for the expedition up the Hudson. Several times he returned to Ireland where at one time he commanded at Belfast, and at another time was M.P. for Charleville, County Cork.

In Britain and in Europe the soldierly Nugents served on many fronts and were awarded innumerable foreign orders. Count Michael Antony Nugent, who died in 1812, was Governor of Prague. His nephew, Count Nugent Lavall, was a Field Marshal in the Austrian army, which he entered as a cadet straight from his Irish home. He was temporarily deprived of his commission because he refused to sign the conditions imposed at the peace conference at the time of Napoleon's marriage to Maria Louisa. At the age of eighty-two he was present at Solferino, as a volunteer.

PLUNKETT

P LUNKETT is a name scarcely heard of outside Ireland unless it applies to Irish exiles. It is of French origin, a corruption of blanchet, from blanc, white, and referring to the fair Plunketts who possibly arrived in Ireland with the Normans. It is a name borne by many distinguished men in church, state, the armed forces and the arts.

The Plunketts settled in north County Dublin, in Meath and Louth. In 1316 there is mention of Thomas Plunkett of Louth who was Chief Justice of the Common Pleas. Sir Christopher Plunkett was Lord of Killeen and in 1628, Lucas, 10th Lord of Killeen was created Earl of Fingall. From Sir Christopher Plunkett, Lord of Killeen, descend also the Barons of Louth and the Earls of Dunsany. Dunsany Castle, one of the finest in Meath, is still the home of the Plunkett family, whose ancestor was created 1st Baron of Dunsany by Henry VI.

Despite Cromwellian and Williamite confiscation and the adherence to the old faith by some branches of the family, the Plunketts, unlike many other important families, managed to retain most of their estates and castles, perhaps because they were peaceably inclined.

On the outbreak of the 1641 rising Christopher Plunkett, 2nd Earl of Fingall, tried to preserve neutrality and was appointed a commissioner to keep the peace. However, when it was seen that his sympathies lay with the Catholic cause he was outlawed and was indicted. No longer peacefully inclined, he was General of Horse at the Battle of Rathmines in 1649 where he was taken prisoner. He died in Dublin Castle shortly afterwards.

Wayside cross at Killeen, County Meath, depicts Thomas Plunket (d.1471), the third son of Christopher, 1st Baron Killeen, with Marion Cruise. Their children are carved on the other three sides

John Plunkett was altogether a different man. Born in Dublin in 1664, he was educated in Vienna by the Jesuits. It seems that for many years he was actively employed as a spy and he was accused of forging letters implicating the Whig party in assassination plots. Dean Swift believed this to be true. In any case, John Plunkett was charged with complicity in a plot to capture the Tower of London and, inevitably, found himself imprisoned there. However, he was released and reached the age of sixty-four before he died in London.

Thomas Plunkett, born in Meath in 1716, went soldiering in the Austrian army. He fought in the Seven Years War and rose steadily, becoming a General and Governor of Antwerp where he died, aged sixty-three.

Blessed Oliver Plunkett

The name Oliver Plunkett is one of the most revered in Ireland. Born at Loughcrew in Meath, he spent many years in Rome where, in 1657, he was Professor of Theology. At Ghent, in 1669, he was appointed Archbishop of Armagh and returned to his Irish See to face a long, slow martyrdom. It has been said: 'His labours in his diocese were unceasing . . . he never had a house of his own and was often glad to eat oakcake and milk.' In 1670 he wrote, 'I am obliged to conceal myself by assuming the name of Captain Brown, wearing a sword and a wig and carrying pistols,'—strange attire for the premier Catholic bishop of Ireland, but these were the Penal days.

When Titus Oates made his false depositions Plunkett was arrested in Dublin, accused of complicity. He was sent to London in 1680 where he was given an unbelievably dishonest trial, charged with having 'compassed the invasion of Ireland by foreign powers'. He was duly hanged, drawn and quartered at Tyburn the following year. His head was returned to Louth where it can be seen in a Drogheda church. The memory of Blessed Oliver—he has not yet been canonized —long outlives the devious men who contrived his ignominious death.

William Conyngham, 1st Baron Plunkett, was born in 1764 in Enniskillen and, like so many of the Plunketts, graduated from Trinity College, Dublin. He became a K.C. and in the trials following the 1798 rising he defended the Sheares brothers, unsuccessfully, for they were both hanged. He courted certain criticism—and got it—when he prosecuted Robert Emmet whose brother, Thomas, was one of his closest friends.

As an M.P. he spoke out strongly against the Union of 1800 and on his appointment as Solicitor General he continued to advocate the cause of Catholic emancipation. From Attorney General he rose to Chief Justice, receiving a peerage in 1827. In 1830 he was Lord Chancellor of Ireland. As Attorney General he had tried to put down the Orange faction, yet he opposed Daniel O'Connell and his Catholic Association, seeing in it, perhaps, the roots of further divisiveness? He was appointed Master of the Rolls in England, but the professional jealousy of the Bar deemed an Irishman to be a foreigner and he resigned almost at once!

He was a splendid orator. Dr. Madden called him 'one of those mighty minds that exalt a nation', and Sir Robert Peel said he was the most eloquent and most reasoning of men to have spoken at Westminster. He died at his house at Old Connaught, Bray, in County Wicklow, at the age of ninety.

William's grandson, David Robert, 1st Baron Rathmore, born in 1839, wrote a *Life of the 1st Lord Plunket*. David Robert, too, graduated from Trinity College, Dublin, as a barrister and became in time Solicitor-General, Paymaster-General and a Commissioner of Works in various Conservative governments. He was raised to the Peerage and in 1919 died, aged eighty, at Greenore, Louth.

The 4th Baron Plunkett, another William Conyngham, was grandson of the first and was Bishop of Meath and later Archbishop of Dublin of the Church of Ireland in the latter half of the nineteenth century.

John Hubert, born in 1801 in Roscommon, graduated in Law from Dublin University. He broke new ground by setting off for Australia where he became a statesman, Solicitor General of New South Wales and a President of the Upper Chamber. Despite the distance which separated him from Ireland, he campaigned vigorously for Catholic emancipation. He died in Melbourne aged sixty-eight.

George Noble Plunkett, born in Dublin in 1851, was a barrister, educated at Clongowes, County Kildare, and in France. He was created a Papal Count by Pope Leo XIII. He wrote poetry and was Director of the Science and Arts Museum in Dublin and was the father of the 1916 leader, Joseph Plunkett, a revolutionary poet and journalist. Joseph Plunkett was one of the founders of the Irish theatre in Dublin's Hardwicke Street. The military plans for the rising of 1916 were drawn up by him and he was a signatory of the Republican Proclamation. He was executed in 1916.

The farmers of Ireland have good reason to remember Sir Horace Plunkett, third son of the 16th Baron Dunsany. He spent his life working for the improvement of agriculture. Living for a decade in Wyoming, he visited Ireland each year. Eventually he returned and helped to organize dairy co-operatives. He was a member of the Congested Districts Board and a Unionist M.P. for Dublin in 1892. In 1922, after the Treaty, he was made a Senator of the Irish Free State. He founded the Irish Agricultural Organization. Although he had constantly laboured to improve the quality of Irish life, his politics were not agreeable to extremists and he suffered shameful intimidation and the burning of his splendid modern home at Foxrock, County Dublin. Ironically, from the refuge of England, he continued to write and work on Irish rural problems. He died in 1932.

Edward Moreton Drax Plunkett, 18th Baron Dunsany (1878–1957), of County Meath, was a patron of letters who himself wrote many books and plays. He gave great encouragement to young Irish writers. Lord Dunsany's best known fiction character is 'Jorkens', a spinner of unlikely yarns in a London Club. Lord Dunsany was interested in supernatural forces and many of his works follow that theme. His neomyths, *The Gods of Pegana*, *The Sword of Welleran*, *The Glittering Gate* and many more, are now regarded as the forerunners of J. R. R. Tolkien's tales. Lord Dunsany's stories have been reprinted and are very popular.

POWER

THAT the name Power is not an impeccably Irish one might surprise many a native Irishman for the Irish Powers are a widespread clan. Originally, in the sixth century, they came from Brittany, via England, and the legends which have accumulated around their name have come down through generations. In Brittany there is a story that a Countess of Poher became the fifth wife of the Count Comorre, the original Bluebeard. She, too, was chopped by him, but she is chronicled as St. Trifine, mother of St. Tremeur of Brittany. Reversing the situation, around 1324, by which time the Powers were settled in Ireland, Sir John de Power risked becoming fourth husband to that notorious husband-consuming witch of Kilkenny, Alice le Kyteler.

Poher, le Poer, Power, the name stems from the French word, povre, pauper, poor. Edward MacLysaght, the genealogist, says, 'the poverty implied was rather that of a voluntary vow than of destitution.' The Powers came to England in 1066, and, a century later, to Ireland with Strongbow. They boasted that among their forebears there was royalty both French and English.

Margaret Power, Countess of Blessington

131

It was with the encouragement of a relative, Henry II of England, that they established themselves in Waterford. He also granted the lands of Lismore and of Baltinglass in County Wicklow to Sir Robert, the Power of that time. It seems possible that it was Sir Robert's son, William, who built the first castle of Powerscourt in County Wicklow which, later, was taken from the Powers by the native O'Tooles. Today the name lives on in Powerscourt Gardens, among the finest in the world.

The le Poers, as some of the lineage were known, acquired many titles; Earl of Tyrone, Count de le Poer Beresford, Marquess of Waterford, to mention a few. They fought, sometimes for, other times against, the kings and queens of England, both at home and on the continent. They were variously imprisoned in Dublin Castle, or executed in the Tower of London, or buried honourably in Westminster Abbey.

It was Henry VIII who conferred the title of Baron le Poer of Curraghmore (County Waterford) on Sir Piers Power, a Sheriff of Waterford. John Power, a generation or two later, entertained Queen Elizabeth's Lord Deputy, Sir Henry Sidney, at Curraghmore. Another of the line favoured James II and took part in the siege of Limerick of which he was Mayor.

Despite treasons, fire and sword, the Powers proliferated, serving their country, not only in the army but also in the church. One was an archbishop of Tuam in 1743, and early in the nineteenth century one of the aristocratic Powers was Archbishop of Armagh and Primate of all Ireland. The clerical Powers are to be found in both the Roman Catholic Church and the Church of Ireland. The Reverend Edmond Power, a Jesuit, wrote learnedly on Islam. The Reverend Patrick Power was an antiquarian and historian. As recently as 1961 the Reverend Michael Power was created first Bishop of Toronto.

The Powers could also wield the pen. 'The most beautiful Countess of Blessington', who began life as Margaret Power of Knockbrit in County Tipperary, earned fame as a biographer of her friend, Byron. With her step-son-in-law, Count D'Orsay, painter and king of the dandies, she was the chatelaine of glittering, all-male, intellectual salons in both London and Paris. When Lord Blessington died, to maintain the splendour and also to support her Power family—her father, old 'shiver-the-frills', was a profligate—she worked ten hours a day, writing. She was in truth the first, full-time woman journalist. Her niece, another Margaret Power, also contributed to the periodicals of her time.

In more recent times, Frank Power of County Leix was a war correspondent. His despatches to *The Times* were sent from Bulgaria, and from Khartoum where he survived the siege. John Power of Waterford was a bibliographer. Albert Power, a sculptor, is famous for his memorial to the sinking of the 'Lusitania' off Cobh during the first world war. An admiral of the British fleet, Sir Arthur Power, has been said by Lord Longford to be 'one of the greatest—some say, last of the old sea dogs'.

Stage and screen have brought notoriety to the far flung Powers. Frederic Tyrone Power, born 1869, played with Henry Irving and died in California in 1931. The great days of Hollywood knew that other Tyrone Power, the much-married, swashbuckling film star.

The Powers have given to Ireland in equal measure what they have taken from it, not least of which is uisce beatha, Irish for 'water of life', i.e. whiskey. In 1771, James Power founded his distillery in John's Lane, Dublin. His son,

W. Tyrone Power (1797–1841), first of a succession of famous actors bearing this name. He was drowned in the sinking of the steamship President.

John, a friend of Daniel O'Connell and a High Sheriff of the City of Dublin, developed it considerably. In the 1870's, when marketing techniques were rudimentary, the company pioneered the miniature liquor bottle. It required a special Act of Parliament to launch the Baby Power, the tiny bottle which caused their Gold Label whiskey to acquire its alias of 'The Three Swallows'. Since then Powers have moved to one of the most modern bottling plants in Europe, at Clondalkin, County Dublin. Today's chairman, an O'Reilly, is a descendant of the Power founder.

The Powers—there are at least 11,000 in Ireland today—are still living mainly in the South West. A glance in the Irish telephone directory will confirm this. A chain of Power bookmakers extends around the country.

The descendants of the Powers who came from Brittany are today scattered far. At Curraghmore, the miniature Versailles they built long ago by the Clodagh River, some miles from Carrick-on-Suir, the 8th Marquess of Waterford, the 12th Baronet, lives with his wife and sons. It is, of course, a treasure house of Power history and legend. The Shell House, which can be visited, was created by Catherine, Countess of Tyrone, who married Sir Marcus Beresford and won an important right for Irish heiresses by succeeding in winning the battle to inherit property through the female line. No wonder her statue in marble is one of the features of the Shell House at Curraghmore.

O'REILLY

O'REILLY is a most Irish name, today found all over Ireland. O'Reillys and O'Rourkes were interconnected by both blood and war. They possessed vast tracts of land in Breffny and O'Reilly's territory at one time included most of County Cavan while during the thirteenth and fourteenth centuries it extended into parts of Meath. In the history of trade in Ireland in medieval times their name is frequently mentioned. They appear to have been adept at commerce— at one time 'reilly' was a term for Irish money. Perhaps they also lived well for there is a saying about someone for whom things go well that 'he's having the life of Reilly'.

The O'Reillys must have branched south for there is mention of the Reillys of Cork being as famed as the Blakes of Galway. One O'Reilly was mayor of Cork. MacRichard Butler, of the great family of Ormond, boasted of his O'Reilly mother.

O'Reilly independence and ownership of land and property lasted until the confiscations of Oliver Cromwell. Ecclesiastically they have always been most distinguished. Since the sixteenth century there have been five O'Reilly Archbishops of Armagh, five bishops of Kilmore, two of Clogher and one of Derry.

The first of these, the Most Reverend Dr. Edmund O'Reilly, born in Dublin in 1606 and educated at Louvain, had a strange career. For a while he was Governor of Wicklow where he was convicted in 1642 of murder. Pardoned, he went abroad to Lille. Twelve years later, at Brussels, he was consecrated Bishop of Armagh. It took him four years to reach Ireland and he had hardly arrived before his authority was withdrawn by the Pope and he was arrested and ordered to leave. He died at Saumur aged sixty-three.

Hugh O'Reilly, a barrister born at Cavan, was a Master in Chambers and a Clerk of the Council under James II in Ireland. He went to France with King James where he received the honorary appointment of Lord Chancellor of Ireland.

Philip MacHugh O'Reilly of Cavan, was married to Owen Roe O'Neill's sister and, with him, was largely responsible for the abortive rising of 1641 for which the Irish paid so dear. He made his last stand at Lough Uachtair in 1652 and was allowed to go abroad where he transferred to the Spanish army. He died in Louvain some years later.

The O'Reillys featured prominently among the military men who put their swords at the disposal of European dynasties when there was no opportunity for using them in the service of their own country. James II's Irish Army included Colonel Edmund O'Reilly's regiment of infantry in which there were thirty-three O'Reilly officers. In Colonel Mahon's regiment, sixteen of the officers bore the name Reilly or O'Reilly. As professional soldiers in the armies on the field in Europe it is possible that O'Reilly may have confronted O'Reilly on opposing sides.

Count Don Alexander O'Reilly was born at Baltrasna, Meath, in 1722. He went first to Spain as a lieutenant in the Irish Brigade. From there he moved on to the Austrian army and distinguished himself in their war against Prussia.

Ballyjamesduff, County Cavan, made famous by the song, 'Come back Paddy Reilly to Ballyjamesduff'

Transferring to the French service, he assisted at the Battle of Bergen in 1759. A thoroughly professional fighting man, he moved on to Spain with promotion to Lieutenant General. In Madrid he saved the life of Charles II and was invited to introduce Germanic discipline to the Spanish army. On achieving Field Marshal status he went on a mission to Havana. In 1768, he took over Louisiana. On his return he became Governor of Madrid. He died at the age of seventy-five near Chincilla, obviously still with strong feelings for his homeland for he is reputed, some years before his death, to have paid an Irish gentleman a thousand guineas for preparing his pedigree.

Count Andrew O'Reilly was another aristocratic fighting Irishman. Born in Ireland in 1740, he was a Field Marshal in the army of Austria during the reign of Maria Theresa. He fought in the seven years war and he served with Joseph II against the Turks. He was taken prisoner by the French at one stage. Freed again he commanded a body of cavalry at Austerlitz and he served also with the Archduke Maximilian. As Governor of Vienna in 1805 he had the humiliating experience of having to surrender Vienna to Napoleon. He died there at the age of ninety-two.

With the approach of the nineteenth century the O'Reillys became less martial. Edward, born in Cavan around 1770, went to live in Dublin, from which unlikely source he managed to publish, by subscription, an Irish-English Dictionary. He also compiled what might be the first dictionary of Irish Writers—he recorded 400 in 1820.

John Roberts O'Reilly deserves particular mention. A Meath man, he entered the navy and in 1814 lost his sight in battle. Despite his blindness he entered the coastguard service where he saved many people from shipwreck. To him goes the credit for inventing the distress flare for which he was made a naval Knight of Windsor. He died in 1873, aged sixty-five.

The Fenian John Boyle O'Reilly is probably the most famous O'Reilly in Ireland since the great Philip MacHugh O'Reilly of Cavan. Born at Dowth, County Meath, in 1844, John Boyle O'Reilly joined the Irish Republican Brotherhood and then enlisted in the British army, intending to sap the strength of its soldiers. He was discovered and was sentenced to death in 1866. However, this was commuted to penal servitude and transportation to Australia. From there he escaped and got to Boston where he edited *The Pilot* and helped plan the escape of six more Fenians. He wrote popular poetry and an extremely successful novel about convict settlements. He died in Boston, aged forty-six.

Of contemporary O'Reillys, Tony O'Reilly the handsome hero of the unbeatable Lions Irish rugby team of the 1960's and, afterwards, an international business magnate, appears to combine the historic fighting and trading characteristics of the O'Reillys.

Tony O'Reilly, Irish rugby player of the 1960's and business magnate extraordinary

O'ROURKE (Rorke)

I N the tenth and eleventh centuries the kingship of Connacht was held by three members of the O'Rourke family. Their name comes from the Norse Hrothrekr, Gaelicized to Ruarc from whom sprang a virile family well recorded in Irish history. Until the confiscations of Cromwell their chieftains were lords of Breffny —at that time parts of Leitrim and Cavan. At the height of their powers the Breffny O'Rourkes ruled from Kells in County Meath to the northern tip of Sligo.

They followed the old unhappy pattern; clan jealously warring against clan, O'Rourkes against O'Reillys. Tiernan O'Rourke (d.1172), chieftain of Breffny, ravaged Meath and killed the king of Meath. He also carried his warfare into Connacht, the territory of the O'Briens and the O'Connors. Dermot Mac-Murrough, King of Leinster, who was also striving to subdue Connacht, there encountered Tiernan O'Rourke's wife, Dervorgilla, and carried her off, with

O'Rourke's Table in County Leitrim, the setting for Thomas Moore's poem, 'The Valley lay smiling before me', in which he recalls Dervorgilla's desertion of her husband, Tiernan O'Rourke

most of her dowry. He eventually had to send her back to O'Rourke. Mac-Murrough had made an implacable enemy. O'Rourke allied himself with O'Conor, king of Connacht, and Dermot MacMurrough was deposed and driven from Ireland. By subsequently seeking the support of King Henry II of England, Mac-Murrough opened the floodgates of the Anglo-Norman invasion.

The O'Rourkes suffered heavily in the Elizabethan wars. Brian O'Rourke, Sir Brian-na-Murtha (of the ramparts), although he was inaugurated O'Rourke in 1564, accepted an English knighthood at Athlone in 1578. Ten years later he had changed his allegiance and is said to have protected many survivors of the Spanish Armada. This was considered a grave offence and he had to flee to Scotland where James VI treacherously handed him over to Elizabeth. Because he could speak no English he refused trial by jury, but was nevertheless condemned to death and he went to the scaffold at Tyburn in 1591.

He was succeeded by his natural son, Brian Og of the Battle Axes who fought

137

in the Nine Years War with the O'Neills and the O'Donnels and was at the siege of Kinsale. He died in 1604 at Galway.

From then onwards the history of the Breffny O'Rourkes is predominantly centred in Europe, where in the church, the state and with the sword, they were distinguished.

Manus O'Rourke (1660–1741), who was educated for the church in Paris, was one of a number of Irish-speaking priests at the Jacobite court at St. Germain-en-Laye.

Eugene O'Rourke also followed James, 'the Old Pretender', to France and was entrusted with the task of sounding out whether the Elector Palatine might consider James for a son-in-law. The Elector was unwilling; nonetheless, the Old Pretender made Eugene O'Rourke his Minister Plenipotentiary at the court of Vienna, where O'Rourke died in 1723.

Because of his princely origin, John O'Rourke, formerly of Leitrim, was given a commission in the Royal Scotch Regiment by Louis XV. His French Colleagues did not like this so he transferred to Russia where, a major in the Czar's regiment of bodyguards, he fought against Prussia and was presented by Frederick the Great with a diamond-studded sword. He later returned to France where he served with the cavalry and was created a Count. He died in Vienna in 1786, aged seventy-six. Interesting papers relating to Count O'Rourke and his family were not long ago discovered in the Record Office at Vienna.

General Count Iosiph Kornilovich O'Rourke who served in the Russian army

Russian army lists of Czarist days record many O'Rourke names. They were also in Poland. In the nineteen-thirties the Bishop of Danzig was an O'Rourke. Irish writers mention meeting officers and ecclesiastics in Russia bearing the O'Rourke name, who spoke no word of Irish or English.

Maria Nikolaevna, Countess Tarnovska, née O'Rourke (b.1877) of Kiev, was the central character in a celebrated trial held in Venice in 1910, attended by correspondents from all over the world. She was sentenced for complicity in the murder of her husband. An historical novel has been written about her by Hans Habe.

The O'Rourkes have had connections with the theatre. Edmund O'Rourke (1814–1879) changed his name to Falconer when he went on the London stage where he was the first Danny Mann in the 'Colleen Bawn'. He also wrote for the theatre.

138

SHERIDAN

I N Irish the name is Ó Sirideáin, which means descendant of Sirideán, but who this Sirideán was is not recorded. What is positive as regards this ancient Gaelic family is that they have not used the O before their name since the seventeenth century, and though they are now widely dispersed through every province, they all originated from County Cavan. They are a most remarkably consistent family of versatile writers.

Denis Sheridan (b.1612), was ordained in 1634. He was a friend of Bishop Bedell who persuaded him to abandon the Catholic priesthood to embrace Protestantism. Together they translated the Bible into Irish.

His son, William Sheridan (1636–1711), was Protestant Bishop of Kilmore.

Then followed a trio of Thomases. Thomas Sheridan (1647–1712), author and Jacobite, was born near Trim in County Meath. This Thomas, who was a Fellow of Trinity College, Dublin, first met James II, then Duke of York, when they were both in Brussels. Thomas served a period in prison for his participation in a 'Popish Plot'. When he was later set free, he was, in 1680, appointed by James II Chief Secretary and Commissioner of the Revenue in Ireland. However, Tyrconnel, the Lieutenant General in Ireland, who had someone else in mind, prevented this appointment. Thomas, who accompanied James II into exile is said to have married his natural daughter. By her Thomas had a daughter and a son.

This son, also Thomas (1684–1746) was tutor to Prince Charles Edward, the Young Pretender. He was one of the Seven Men of Moidart at the Battle of Falkirk. After Culloden he escaped to Rome where he wrote *Some Revelations of Irish History*.

His nephew, the Chevalier Michael Sheridan (c.1715–1775), also took part in the 'Forty-five Rebellion'.

Thomas Sheridan (1687–1738) born in Cavan and possibly a grandson of Denis, was a pensioner of Trinity College, Dublin. He married Elizabeth, the only child of Charles MacFadden of Quilca House, County Cavan. Originally a Sheridan property, this house was taken from them by King William and given to the MacFaddens. Thomas, a clergyman, opened a school at the King's Mint House in Capel Street, Dublin, for the sons of the best families. When Jonathan Swift came to Dublin as Dean of St. Patrick's Cathedral, Thomas Sheridan's reputation as a schoolmaster was very high. He was no mean scholar. He and Dean Swift became close friends and Swift stayed regularly with him when he went to Quilca, although the Dean found it far from comfortable.

Thomas Sheridan could be extremely absent-minded. On the Sunday following the death of Queen Anne, the text he chose for his sermon was 'sufficient unto the day is the evil thereof', which caused him to be accused of Jacobinism and to be struck off the Chaplain's list. This was a serious deprivation, but his good friend the Dean of St. Patrick's helped him obtain a living near Cork. By fulfilling an old promise to tell the Dean if he ever saw in him signs of avarice, he unwittingly ended their friendship. It was a sad parting, and lacking the Dean's influence, he sank into poverty.

His son, Thomas Sheridan (1719–1788) who was born in Dublin, became one of the most famous actors of his time. In 1747 he was manager of the Theatre Royal, Dublin. He married Frances Chamberlaine who, despite her father's embargo on allowing her any education, was secretly coached by her brother. She became a considerable novelist and dramatist and an ardent supporter of her actor husband. Thomas was also deeply involved in writing and in evolving a new system of education. With the opening of Spranger Barry's theatre in Dublin playgoers were attracted away from the Sheridan theatre. This was a serious loss which meant the Sheridans had to go to England where Thomas began again, this time lecturing on elocution which had always been a great interest of his.

Thomas Sheridan (1719–1788), actor and elocutionist

His son, Richard Brinsley Sheridan (1751–1816) was born in Dublin and educated at Harrow. He married Elizabeth Ann, the very young daughter of the musical composer, Thomas Linley of Bath. With no income and no capital he managed to make his way into fashionable London and he eventually made a tremendous success with his comedy, *The Rivals*. Afterwards, in partnership with others, he bought the Drury Lane Theatre. In it he put on *The School for Scandal* and, in 1779, *The Critic*, all outstandingly popular plays.

Then this master of the comedy of manners turned to politics and for the next thirty years held ministerial posts. He took a major share in the impeachment of Warren Hastings. His parliamentary leader and friend was James Fox and he was also a friend of the Prince Regent. Richard Brinsley Sheridan's wife,

Richard Brinsley Sheridan (1751–1861), master of comedy and M.P.

the former Miss Linley, was a fine singer, and a beauty who was pursued by the nobility because of her good looks and charm. She was also a competent wife who helped not only with his accounts but took an interest in his politics. After her death in 1792 he married a rather less gifted woman. His last days were a series of decline. Drury Lane burned down; James Fox died; Sheridan lost his seat in Parliament. Nonetheless, he was accorded a splendid funeral in Westminster Abbey.

His son, Thomas Sheridan (1775–1817), was a poet of some merit who went to the Cape of Good Hope to take up an appointment in the colonial administration. He died there at an early age, leaving six children. His wife, Caroline, was a novelist whose books were very popular. She gave her three beautiful daughters as good an education as her three handsome sons. Helen Selena (1807–1868), the daughter who became Lady Dufferin, was the song writer who composed the well-known and often sung ballad, *The Irish Emigrant*. Lady Dufferin also wrote amusingly of her travels in Africa and Europe.

Her daughter Caroline married at nineteen the Honourable George Norton, a barrister. He proved to be a poor husband and she had too often to support him and their children by her writing. In 1836, in a bid to acquire what money and effects she had earned from her novels, he falsely accused Lord Melbourne of having an affair with her. Lord Melbourne was acquitted but this incident led to her becoming the original of Meredith's *Diana of the Crossways*.

Caroline Norton (née Sheridan), writer and early campaigner for women's rights

Caroline, a most independent-minded woman at a time when this attitude was not considered feminine, shocked fashionable London by her social consciousness and by publishing a book demanding the rights of women to their own property, and equal rights before the Courts of Justice. It was one of the first of the campaigns which eventually led to a greatly needed re-assessment of justice towards women.

Joseph Sheridan LeFanu (1814–1873) was also of the Sheridans. His father, descended from a Huguenot family, married a relative of Richard Brinsley Sheridan. Joseph Sheridan LeFanu wrote sixteen ghostly novels, the best known of these are *The House by the Churchyard*, *Uncle Silas* and *In a Glass Darkly*.

In Wyoming, U.S.A., there is a town called Sheridan, and there is a Sheridan buried in America's National Cemetery at Arlington. He was General Philip Henry Sheridan, a Union Soldier, the son of a County Cavan exile, who became Commander-in-Chief of the U.S. Army.

The literary tradition of the Sheridans continues with Niall Sheridan, born in County Meath in 1912. He graduated from University College, Dublin, in 1934, a vintage year for poets and writers. His colleagues there included Denis Devlin, Charles Donnelly, Donagh MacDonagh and the great satirist and humorist, Brian Nolan (alias Flann O'Brien, alias Myles na Gopaleen of the *Irish Times*). Niall Sheridan has published *20 Poems 34* and has contributed poetry and short stories to magazines and his play *Seven Men and a Dog* was put on at the Abbey in 1958. He works for Irish Television. His wife, Monica Sheridan, also a writer and television personality, has written books on Irish cooking.

O'SULLIVAN

O 'SULLIVAN is the third most numerous name in Ireland. Súil is the Irish word for eye and it could be that Súildhubhán was descriptive of the early, black-eyed Sullivans, although the scholars are divided about this derivation. The O'Sullivans, from earliest times, were a powerful Munster family, on a par with the MacCarthys and the O'Callaghans. They made their homes originally in Tipperary, later branching out towards Cork and Kerry. The senior Sullivan, O'Sullivan Mor, had his castle at Kenmare, while the next in importance, O'Sullivan Beare, had his castle of Dunboy overlooking Bantry Bay, one of the finest harbours in Ireland. Today it is an oil storage depot.

Between the ceremonious opening of this international commercial project, and the tragic dispersal of the family of Donal O'Sullivan Beare (1560–1618), lies a wealth of Irish history. The story of O'Sullivan Beare is an epic that awaits an Irish Homer. Following the disastrous battle of Kinsale which changed forever the fate of Ireland, although the surrender terms had included all the Irish garrisons, Donal O'Sullivan Beare, who had been given command of the south by O'Neill and O'Donnell, managed to wrest Dunboy back with a garrison of a hundred and forty-three men, including a few Spaniards. Carew, with four thousand men, assaulted it from the sea and from the land. For twenty-one days it held out until hardly a stone was left, and then, while O'Sullivan Beare was away meeting the Spanish ship which had landed too late on the Kerry side of the peninsula, his Constable MacGeoghegan, already mortally wounded, was finally killed as he attempted to fire the gunpowder which would blow up the entire fortress. Every man, woman and child in the castle was slain by Carew and his men. O'Sullivan Beare decided to fight his way north to Leitrim, where he had an ally in O'Rourke.

At the end of December 1602 with four hundred fighting men and six hundred civilians, they began their two-hundred-mile walk. It was two weeks of appalling hardship and bitter tragedy. The Four Masters in their Annals said of O'Sullivan, 'He was not a day or night during this period without a battle, or being vehemently and vindictively pursued; all of which he sustained and responded to with manliness and vigour.' Sadly, his main enemies were Irish chieftains anxious to win approval from their new masters.

From day to day the exodus struggled on, by Ballyvourney, Duhallow, Ardpatrick Solloghod, Ballynakill, Latteragh and Loughkeen. At the wide Shannon river they killed some of their horses and sailed across with boats made from the skins strengthened with osiers. At Aughrim they were attacked by the Anglo-Irish. They fought back and killed both their leaders, Sir Thomas Burke and Captain Malby. Eventually, they reached Brian O'Rourke's castle of Leitrim. Of the original one thousand who had set out, only thirty-five reached Leitrim.

When Elizabeth I died, James I came to the throne and the Irish chieftains, full of hope, went to London, but they had no welcome there from James and no restitution of their territories, so many of them began to go abroad.

Donal O'Sullivan Beare, whose wife and children had been guarded by the MacSweeneys, took flight with his family to Spain in 1604. Here Philip III

Donal O'Sullivan Beare (1560–1618), gallant leader though finally exiled in Spain

treated him most kindly, created him Knight of St. James and Count of Bear-haven and gave him a pension of three hundred pieces of gold monthly. Fourteen years later, aged fifty-eight, he was accidentally killed in an affray in Madrid. Donal, his son, died during the siege of Belgrade. Dermot, his brother, and Dermot's wife, both of whom had been on the march from Dunboy to Leitrim, also went to Spain with their family. Dermot lived to be a hundred years of age.

Dermot, formerly Lord of Dursey Castle at the entrance to Bantry Bay, had a son, Philip, who had been in Spain since childhood. Together with other Irish youths he had been sent a hostage, for the kings of Spain were sending no aid to Ireland without collateral. Philip O'Sullivan Beare was destined for the Spanish navy and he served it faithfully, even if his mind was more equably engaged in the study of Latin, of history and polemics. Fortunately for the historians, he has left behind, in Latin, a most useful contemporary reference book of the Elizabethan period in Ireland.

From now on, the story of the O'Sullivans is diffuse, pinpointed with characters pursuing diverse careers, at home, in the old world and the new. The poets and the writers preponderate. In Cleeve's dictionaries of Irish Writers there are no less than fifteen, up until the present day.

Owen Roe O'Sullivan (1748–1784), the poet, was born in Kerry where he gave up his farm labouring to use his education for teaching in a school. His weakness for women, and they for him, disordered his life so that he had to abandon school-mastering. For a while he was in the British navy, sailing to and from the West Indies. Then he changed to the army from which he escaped back to school-teaching. All the time he wrote the poems and the songs which linger on long after his death. He has come to be regarded as a great lyric poet.

Tadhg Gaolach O'Sullivan (1715–1795) was born in Kerry a little earlier, lived considerably longer, and had none of the disarming wickedness of Owen Roe. His poems were mostly Jacobite political, or sentimentally religious. Dr. Douglas Hyde, the Gaelic scholar, has described them as 'very musical and mellifluous'.

Clergymen can be invaluable archivists. The O'Sullivans have had churchmen of distinction including many bishops. Mortimer O'Sullivan (1791–1859) born in Clonmel to Catholic parents, changed to Protestantism and became a clergyman. He wrote vigorously against landlordism. Mortimer O'Sullivan's most lasting work was his *Digest of Evidence on the State of Ireland* which was published in 1826. He was the first head master of the Royal School at Dungannon, County Tyrone.

His brother, Samuel (c.1790–1851), also a convert to the Established Church, was Chaplain to the Military School at the Phoenix Park, Dublin.

From the seventeenth century the O'Sullivans branched out into various countries of Europe. John O'Sullivan (1700–1746) was born in Kerry and was sent to Paris and Rome to be educated for the priesthood, but, changing his mind, he returned to Ireland. The Penal Laws presented him with the choice of forfeiting his estates, or changing his religion. He returned to France where he entered the army and saw much service, and earned a reputation as a guerilla fighter. When Prince Charles Stuart was planning his assault upon Scotland in 1745, John O'Sullivan was chosen as his Adjutant and Quarter-Master-General. From then until Prince Charles' escape after Culloden on a French frigate— captained by another Irishman, Antoine Walsh—John O'Sullivan was by his side. Despite the debacle, he was knighted afterwards for his services by 'James III', the Old Pretender.

Thomas, John O'Sullivan's son, was also an army officer. He served in three armies, those of America, Britain and Holland where he died in 1823 with the rank of major.

The account of two brothers who were in France at the time of the Revolution is a violent one. Charles O'Sullivan, grandson of an Irish emigré who had settled at Nantes, was a royalist. He had saved his brother John, an ardent revolutionary, from the militant Vendéans. Later, John, a former fencing master, became a most notorious terrorist. With the Pro-Consul, Carrier, he organized the inhuman sinking of the barges filled with priests and other citizens—a diabolic way of bypassing the slowness of the guillotine and the expense of gunfire. John even betrayed his own royalist brother, Charles, who was guillotined. When the inevitable revulsion to the terror set in, John O'Sullivan came before the Revolutionary Tribunal who found him guilty of many cruelties and murders, but set him free 'because he did not act with criminal revolutionary intention'. He was merely 'a revolutionary with a perverted moral sense'.

Morty Og O'Sullivan was a dispossessed member of the O'Sullivans of Berehaven who became a Captain in the Irish Brigade in France. He served in the army of Maria Theresa of Austria and he was at the Battle of Fontenoy in 1745. A year later he, too, was one of the numerous Irishmen supporting Prince Charles Stuart at Culloden. After that defeat he went to sea to earn his living, smuggling from the conveniently indented Munster coast to and from France. He also smuggled 'wild geese', young men escaping from the frustrations of English rule in Ireland, to join the Irish Brigade in France. England had also forbidden the export of Irish wool. Morty Og personally exported it to France to finance his adventures. Eventually, he was caught and shot dead. Many ballads have been written in remembrance of Morty Og O'Sullivan.

In the nineteenth century the O'Sullivan name is frequently encountered in the records of the British navy and it includes one Victoria Cross, awarded to John O'Sullivan of Bantry. There were four Admirals in one family who spelt their name Sulivan.

In the United States of America also, the Sullivan name began to appear with great vitality and versatility. General John O'Sullivan (1744–1808) was to the forefront in the American War of Independence. He opened the hostilities by capturing a fort and taking a cannon. He was a personal friend of George Washington and, at the siege of Boston, he watched the English sail away. A lawyer by profession, both he and his brother James, also a lawyer, gave good service in the setting up of the new nation. James was twice elected Governor of Massachusetts. There were, in fact, four Sullivan boys, all the sons of an emigrant gentleman from Limerick. The Sullivan name features prominently in the topography of the United States of America.

John Lawrence Sullivan (1858–1918) was born in Boston of parents who had come from Tralee. His father was a small man. His mother weighed 180 pounds and from her John Sullivan undoubtedly got his prodigious physique which led him to become one of the most famous pugilists in sporting history. He began to live riotously until he sank to vaudeville appearances. His second wife reformed him and he concluded his days as a temperance lecturer.

Louis Henri Sullivan (1856–1924) always referred to himself as 'of mongrel origin'. His Irish father was a musician who, in the course of his European wanderings, married a French/German wife. In Chicago, where they lived in his youth, Louis Henri had the benefit of grandparents of three nationalities. He became one of Chicago's most memorable architects, pursuing his 'form follows function' theory to Europe and back again. He designed the Auditorium and many other of Chicago's very splendid public buildings.

James Edward Sullivan (1860–1914), whose parents came from Kerry, made his way by self-education to success as a publisher. He had a passionate interest in the promotion of amateur sport. He pioneered the Amateur Athletic Union of the United States, and it was his idea to start New York's Public School Athletic League. He also opened the first public playground there. He was American Director of the Olympic Games and he personally represented President Theodore Roosevelt and President Taft at the Olympic Games from 1906 to 1912.

Two Irish-Canadians feature among the Sullivans in north America. William Henry Sullivan (1864–1929) began as a lumberman and became a civic leader. Born of Irish parents at Port Dalhousie, Ontario, he moved on to the United States, to Louisiana where he formed and named the town of Bogalusa and also served it once as mayor.

Allihies on the Beara Peninsula, County Cork—O'Sullivan country

Joseph Anthony Sullivan (1886–1972) was Roman Catholic bishop of Kingston, Ontario.

In Britain, today, the O'Sullivans are numerous. Bernard John (1915) is a sporting journalist, one of the leading writers on thoroughbred breeding and racing.

Right Reverend Monsignor James O'Sullivan (1917) is the Principal Roman Catholic Chaplain of the British army since 1969. Born in Cork, he has carried out his duties in Normandy, Malaya and Berlin.

In Ireland, poets, scholars, politicians add lustre to the O'Sullivan name.

John Marcus O'Sullivan (1891–1948) was from Killarney and achieved his Doctorate of Philosophy at Heidelberg in 1906. He was Professor of Modern History at University College, Dublin. In 1926 he entered the Dail as Deputy for North Kerry and was successively Parliamentary Secretary to the Minister for Finance and from 1926 until 1932, when the Fine Gael party was defeated by De Valera, he was Minister for Education. He had a very European outlook and went frequently as a delegate to the United Nations. William T. Cosgrave, head of the Free State government, described him as 'a most loyal and able Minister and a great humanist'.

Donal O'Sullivan, born in Liverpool in 1893 of Kerry parents, was a naval officer in the first world war. He has been an Irish Senator and a President of the Irish Council of the European Movement. He wrote knowledgeably about Irish Folk music and musicians long before the arrival of 'pop' folk. He edited *The Bunting Collection of Irish Folk Music.*

Séan O'Súilleabháin, born in County Kerry in 1903, is known internationally as a folklorist. He has done much research abroad and is Registrar and Archivist for the Irish Folklore Commission.

Muris Ó'Súileabháin (1904–1950) was born on the Great Blasket Island off County Kerry where he became fluent in Irish and English. He joined the Civic Guards and while stationed in Connemara he wrote *Fiche Blian ag Fás*, which, translated as 'Twenty Years a-Growing', was reprinted and translated into many languages. It is a simple story of his childhood on the islands.

Daniel James O'Sullivan who was born in County Cork in 1906, worked as a lighthouse keeper and has written *Lightkeepers' Lyrics*. He is also a naturalist and a short story writer.

TAAFFE

T AAFFE is a Welsh name signifying David, and the family came from Wales to Ireland in 1196 shortly after the Anglo-Norman invasion. The founder of the family was Sir Nicholas Taaffe whose grandson, Richard Taaffe, was Sheriff of Dublin in 1295, and also a Sheriff of County Louth.

John Taaffe, son of Richard Taaffe, was a Franciscan and Archbishop of Armagh. The Taaffe family filled many priestly and civic offices.

As was not unusual in medieval times, they fought on opposite sides on different occasions. Sir William Taaffe's branch of the family had moved to Ballymote, Sligo, where he was Sheriff in 1588. Fighting on the government side he distinguished himself in the O'Neill wars. After the siege of Kinsale, when the Spaniards and the native Irish were routed, William received his knighthood, but, to quote the accounts of the time, 'had not the least share in the ensuing confiscation of the territory of the MacCarthys'. He died in 1630.

His son, Sir John Taaffe, was the 1st Baron Ballymote and 1st Viscount Taaffe —he was created a peer in 1628.

His eldest son, Theobald Taaffe (d.1677) of Ballymote, was M.P. for County Sligo in 1639 and became the 2nd Viscount Taaffe. Differing from his grandfather, Sir William, he joined the Confederation at Kilkenny and commanded their forces in Connacht and Munster. Murrough O'Brien (Lord Inchiquin) defeated the Catholic Confederate army at Knocknanoss in 1647 near Mallow in County Cork. After the restoration, Theobald was created the 1st Earl of Carlingford, taking his title from the County Louth town where Taaffe's Castle, the family stronghold, can still be seen.

His brother, Lucas, was also in the army of the Confederates and was Governor of New Ross, County Wexford, in 1649.

The Taaffes ardently supported the Jacobites. Nine Taaffes were in the army of James II in 1690. Nicholas, son of Theobald and 2nd Earl of Carlingford, was killed at the battle of the Boyne, and his brother, John, died at the siege of Derry.

The migration to Austria began with Francis, 3rd Earl of Carlingford and 4th Viscount Taaffe. In the service of Austria he was chamberlain to the Emperor Ferdinand, a Marshal of the Empire and a Councillor-of-State. He died in 1704 and the Carlingford title became extinct with the death of his nephew, Theobald, the 4th Earl.

Nicholas, a collateral descendant of Francis', was 6th Viscount Taaffe (1677–1752). He was born at O'Crean's Castle in County Sligo and he, too, entered the Austrian service and rose to Field Marshal. He fought against the Turks and took a prominent part in agitation for Catholic Emancipation in Ireland. Because of 'his unchanging attachment to an unfortunate country', he was described as 'the German statesman and general, the Irish sufferer and patriot'. Although he succeeded to the title, his Irish estates were gone. Among his many distinctions was that of introducing the potato to Silesia. He died at his seat of Ellischau in Bohemia in 1769.

The Taaffe's had had many castles in Ireland; Smarmore Castle at Ardee in

Nicholas, 6th Viscount Taaffe (1677–1769), Count of the Holy Roman Empire, German statesman and Irish patriot

County Louth, and Ballymote in Sligo, Taaffe's Castle at Carlingford, and several others. In Bohemia, until comparatively recently, they had their seats at Ellischau and Kolinetz. Despite the distinguished careers they pursued in Austria their adopted country, they never lost touch with the British Isles. In 1860, the 10th Viscount Taaffe established, before the British House of Lords, his right to his Irish title. Nobility was a very potent force in court and army circles.

His brother, Edward (1833–1895) the 11th Viscount Taaffe, was Imperial Prime Minister of Austria for fourteen years and among the many orders he held was that of Knight of the Golden Fleece, one of the most distinguished orders in Christendom. He was also Baron of Ballymote in the peerage of Ireland. He was born in Vienna and as a child was one of the chosen companions of the future Emperor, Franz Joseph (1830–1916). All his life he enjoyed the unlimited confidence of the Emperor. There were those who thought him 'essentially an opportunist' maintaining himself in office by the unprecedented employment of the principle, '*divide et impera*'. He was disliked by the Crown Prince Rudolph, a frustrated progressive who was stifled by the autocracy of the imperial court. After the tragedy of Mayerling, when Rudolph and the young Marie Vetsera died together, the Emperor Franz Joseph entrusted the documents of the case to Count Taaffe rather than to the Austrian archives. He imposed a heavy burden of secrecy, not only on Count Edward Taaffe, but also on succeeding generations.

His son Heinrich, the 12th Viscount Taaffe, was removed from the roll of Viscounts because he fought against Britain in the first world war. His son, Eduard Karl Richard (1898–1967) used only his imperial title, Count Taaffe. In 1931 he came to Dublin, married an Irish woman and returned to his estates which, after the war, were in Czechoslovak territory. In 1937 they were

Edward (1833–1895), 11th Viscount Taaffe, Imperial Prime Minister of Austria for fourteen years, and Baron of Ballymote in Ireland

confiscated and he returned to Ireland. He was entered as a candidate for the office of President of the Irish State, but Professor Douglas Hyde, the Gaelic scholar, was considered a more suitable appointment.

All his life Count Eduard Taaffe had been the target for enquiries about the Mayerling documents. In 1929 Randolph Hearst offered him $200,000, and there were many more tempting offers and, though stricken by poverty towards the end of his days, he died leaving unanswered all questions concerning the death of the Crown Prince. And so, with Count Eduard Taaffe, the 13th Viscount, the famous Austrian line became extinct.

There were, of course, other Taaffes. When Dr. Edward O'Reilly, the Primate of Ireland, was forcibly exiled in 1666 because of the Penal Code restricting Roman Catholics, a Father James Taaffe conceived the daring scheme of getting the Irish church under his absolute control. He forged a Bull from the Holy See, making him Vicar Apostolic of all Ireland with power to do almost as he pleased with the diocesan priests and Bishops. He was exposed and duly dealt with in 1668.

The Reverend Denis Taaffe (1753–1813) of County Louth, a Catholic clergyman, was educated in Prague and was sent to Ireland on a mission. His disorderly habits obliged his superior to excommunicate him, so he became a Protestant minister. He joined the United Irishmen and fought in Wexford. He helped found the Gaelic Society and published a history of Ireland and wrote many political pamphlets. He died in Dublin, having been reconciled to the Catholic church.

John Taaffe (1787–1862) born in County Louth, was a poet, a friend of Byron and of Shelley. He published many poems and stories and is best remembered as a commentator on Dante. He died at Fano in Italy.

There are many Taaffes in various parts of Ireland today including 'Toss' Taaffe, a leading Irish jockey whose name will always be associated with that superb Irish horse, 'Arkle'.

O'TOOLE

THE O'Tooles were one of the great Leinster septs. Their surname comes from Tuathal, King of Leinster who died in 956. Tuathal, according to Father Woulfe, means prosperous, and that the O'Tooles undoubtedly were. They possessed the southern half of the rich plains of County Kildare from which they were driven by the Anglo-Norman usurpers in 1172. With their neighbours in North Kildare, the O'Byrnes, they sought shelter in the Wicklow hills and valleys where they held their own for over five hundred years, becoming a very mighty people.

They had their castles at Imail, now Talbotstown, at Castlekevin, Annamoe and Powerscourt which was then called Fearcuallann. During the reign of James I the whole of the lands at Fearcuallann was confiscated from the O'Tooles and was granted to Sir Richard Wingfield with whose family it remained until a short while ago.

'To the Anglo-Norman colonists of the twelfth century, the O'Tooles and the O'Byrnes were veritable ultramontanes,' says John O'Toole, who wrote a history of his family early this century. They were fighting men and they were holy men—some of them. Saint Laurence O'Toole, born about 1130, became the first

ARTHURUS SEVERUS O-TOOLE NONESUCH: Ætatis 80.

'Great Mogul's Landlord, of both Indies King,
Whose self-admiring fame doth loudly ring;
Writes fourscore Years, more Kingdoms he hath right to,
The Stars say so, and for them he will fight too:
And though this worthless Age will not believe him,
But clatter, spatter, slander, scoff, to grieve him;
Yet He and all the World in this agree,
That such another Toole will never be.'

Publish'd by W. Richardson, Castle Street, Leicester Fields

151

Irish archbishop of Dublin. Son of Murtough, a Chieftain of Kildare, his mother was an O'Byrne of a kindred tribe. He was only twelve when his grandfather was killed by Dermot MacMurrough who took the child hostage. His father rescued him and sent him to the monastery of Glendalough where he is reported to have practised remarkable austerities. At twenty-five he became ruler of this very important settlement which, to this day, is a place of pilgrimage.

During Laurence O'Toole's reign as Archbishop of Dublin it was captured by his old enemy, MacMurrough. There was also dissension between Strongbow and the other leading chieftains, and also with Henry II of England to whom, eventually, the Irish chieftains submitted, though not happily.

Meanwhile, to intercede for his country with a more objective authority, Bishop Laurence O'Toole set off for Rome to see Pope Alexander II. He got no further than Normandy where, at Eu, he died from fever on 14th November 1180. He was the first Irishman who lived in Ireland to receive papal canonization.

There was another Wicklow O'Toole, not so revered in Ireland. Adam Duff O'Toole adopted views similar to those afterwards held by Wycliffe's followers. 'His offence was aggravated by the charge of horrid and senseless blasphemy.' He was pronounced a heretic and was burned alive in 1327 near St. Andrew's church in Dublin's Suffolk Street.

Glendalough, County Wicklow, was where St. Laurence O'Toole (born c. 1130), the first Irish archbishop of Dublin, founded a monastery

Glendalough and the valley of the Dargle has been O'Toole country for centuries. A carved stone head, supposed to represent a king of the O'Tooles, is looked after in the world-famous gardens of Powerscourt House, one of the former strongholds of the O'Tooles. Across this vast territory which stretched to Glendalough they fought with, or against, O'Byrnes, Kavanaghs, MacMurroughs, and were ravaged by Norman, Dane and Saxon. It could well have been an O'Toole who, at Bray by the sea, killed the only Romans who, it is thought, ever attempted an Irish landing.

Three-and-a-half centuries after Saint Laurence O'Toole had gone to inter-

Peter O'Toole, film star

cede with the Pope about the Saxon invaders, Tirlogh O'Toole parleyed with Henry VIII's deputy at his castle of Fassaroe near Bray in County Wicklow. But, eventually, like all the other Irish chieftains, they were driven from their country. No less than the other emigrés, the O'Tooles distinguished themselves in the European wars, many of them as officers in the Irish Brigade in the service of France.

When Sir Charles Wogan of Dillon's Regiment of the Irish Brigade in France rescued Princess Clementina, grand-daughter of John Sobieski, King of Poland, from parental confinement in Innsbruck he was assisted ably by Luke O'Toole. Overcoming great difficulties they got her to Italy where, at Bologna, she married the Old Pretender to whom she had been affianced, against the wishes of her family, two years previously. For this daring abduction, which became the subject of many novels, Luke O'Toole was decorated by Pope Clement XI.

Luke O'Toole was guillotined during the Terror. So, also, was his kinsman, Laurence O'Toole who was born in Wexford in 1722. They were all officers in the Irish Brigade in France and the descendants of Laurence O'Toole remained there as Counts O'Toole of Limoges.

On the feminine side little is recorded. Rose O'Toole, a sister of the O'Toole chieftain at Castlekevin, married the famous warrior Fiach McHugh O'Byrne (d.1597) q.v.

Bryan O'Toole, a Lieutenant Colonel in the regiment of English Hussars who fought on the battlefields of Europe, mostly against France, wrote comical letters home to his mother and to his sweetheart, Norah, in County Wexford.

'Norah,' he wrote, 'lived convenient to his mother,' which was why 'the noshuns of Bryan O'Toole on the goings on of the "Irishtocracy" in London', went all in the one letter. About London's annual Royal Academy Exhibition he wrote pages of shrewd, humorous criticism. What happened to his Norah is hard to discover, but he was home long enough to fight at Vinegar Hill and the battle of Ballinahinch. He died in 1825, having fought in Italy and Spain, losing an arm in the Peninsular service.

Sometimes the O is dropped from the name. Laurence Toole (1874–1957) went to Kenora, Ontario, Canada, where the Toole family is a prominent one. George Archer Toole in 1917 was Mayor of Kenora.

There are several distinct O'Toole families. A branch settled in West Connacht and they are also in Mayo, Galway and Ulster.

Perhaps the best known of today's O'Tooles is Peter, the actor and film star.

WALSH

WALSH, or in Irish Breathnach, is a name now so numerous in Ireland, and so widespread, that it seems hard to accept that its origins are not Irish at all, but Welsh. The name MacBratney, meaning in Irish the son of the Welshman, is an Ulster form of this very common surname, of which there are several quite distinct families.

The chief characteristic of the Walsh family in Ireland, or when they went abroad, is the continuing series of churchmen bearing the Walsh name.

William Walsh, a very famous bishop of Meath, was appointed to this important office in 1554. However when Queen Elizabeth asked him to conform, he refused, and for this he was imprisoned and deprived of his bishopric. When released he was brave enough to protest loudly that he would not bow to the politics of the state religion. This meant for him another long term of imprisonment from which, after seven years, he escaped to France. There he took up his priestly duties once more until he was ordered by Rome to act, not only for his former diocese of Meath, but also for Armagh and Dublin. It must have been an exceedingly difficult tenure and eventually he exchanged it to become suffragan Archbishop of Toledo. He died in Spain in 1577.

Nicholas Walsh, Bishop of Ossory, was the son of the Protestant Bishop of Waterford. He was educated at Paris and Cambridge and was consecrated in 1567. He had a progressive turn of mind which led to the introduction of Irish type so that the Protestant Church services could now be printed in Irish, 'which proved an instrument of conversion to many of the ignorant sort of Papists in those days', which was surely one of his objectives. Nicholas Walsh also helped put the New Testament into Irish. In 1585 he was stabbed to death by a man he had publicly accused of adultery. He was buried at St. Canice's, Kilkenny.

Peter Walsh (1618–1688) was a Franciscan. He was born at Moortown, County Kildare, and educated at Louvain. When he returned to Ireland in 1646 he joined the Ormond party which was opposed to the Papal Nuncio, Rinuccini, and the Catholic Confederation. He was disciplined by the Franciscans after he had published his famous Loyal Remonstrance which he addressed to Charles II. In it he repudiated Papal infallibility and promised allegiance from Irish Catholics to the English crown. He hoped to alleviate some of the disabilities the Catholics were forced to endure, but Rome would have none of it. He went to London where he involved himself in much verbal and literary controversy. D'Arcy McGee said of his pamphlet *War*: 'Without it the Catholic Confederacy could not be well understood by our times, or rescued from misrepresentation by the lovers of true history.' The Bishop of Salisbury said of Peter Walsh, among other things, 'He was an honest and able man, much practised in intrigues.' He died in 1688 in London where he had lived on the pension accorded to him by his good friend, James, Earl of Ormond, Lord Lieutenant of Ireland, a member of the eminent Butler family.

Thomas Walsh was born at Ballylin, Limerick, in 1730, where, at eighteen, he started school-teaching. Wesley was touring Ireland at this time and Thomas Walsh joined him and, according to J. Morgan, his biographer, 'became a

154

rousing preacher in Irish and English, remarkably conversant with the Greek Testament and Hebrew Scriptures'. But he wore himself out and died, aged only twenty-eight.

Robert Walsh of Waterford was educated at Trinity College, Dublin, and in 1820 was Chaplain to the British Consulate at Constantinople. Antiquities were his special interest and he managed to combine his hobby with his profession by writing, among other works, *An Essay on Ancient Coins, Medals and Gems as Illustrating the Progress of Christianity in the Early Ages*. He died about 1852.

This is to mention but a few of the many Walshes who have distinguished themselves in the service of the church. Abroad mention must be made of the renowned Abbé Walsh who was the Superior of the Irish College in Paris which was invaded several times by the revolutionary mob. For the Abbé Walsh there were problems for he and his fellow priests were inclined to be royalists, while some of the students were for the Revolution. Matters were further complicated by the fact that the Abbé Walsh had been forcefully appointed Superior by his cousin, Count Walsh de Serrant, a loyalist who led the Irish Regiment of Walsh and whose family had settled at Nantes several generations earlier.

In North America there have been a number of high church dignatories from the Walsh family. John Walsh (1830–1898) was born at Mooncoin, County Kilkenny. He was educated at Toronto where he eventually became Catholic Archbishop. During his administration he established many new churches, schools and charitable institutions. He also kept in touch with Irish politics and had the idea of trying to heal the Parnell split by holding an Irish Race Convention in Dublin.

In 1809 Henry Walsh (1784–1844) of County Antrim was seized by a press gang in Belfast and served in the British navy for six eventful years. He wrote his memoirs prefaced by this sketch of H.M.S. Alfred, on which he first sailed to the West Indies.

In the medical field, the Walshes are also prominent. Edward Walsh (1756–1832), son of the Reverend Robert Walsh and brother of John Edward Walsh, a judge and a one-time Master of the Rolls in Ireland, was a physician and an author. He served with the forces in Ireland, and also in the Peninsular and Waterloo battlefields. He wrote verse and was the founder of the Waterford Literary Society.

Walter Hoyle Walsh (1812–1892) of Kilkenny practised medicine in London where he was a professor at London University. He first described the anatomy of the floating kidney.

Maurice Walsh the novelist (1879–1964)

There were memorable poets: John Walsh, a Gaelic poet of the seventeenth century; Edward Walsh, born in Derry in 1805, who lost his job as a National School teacher because he wrote for *The Nation*, the Fenian newspaper. He got another teaching post, at the detention centre at Spike Island, County Cork. He lost this, too, because he waved farewell to the Fenian, John Mitchell, who was being transported through Cork harbour.

In the army, the navy, and as administrators and consular officials, the Walshes are well documented. Antoine Vincent Walsh (1703–1763), son of Philip (d.1708), a Waterford shipbuilder who had settled at St. Malo, was in charge of the ship which landed Charles Edward Stuart, the Young Pretender, in Scotland in 1745. For this he was knighted. He was yet another of the Irishmen who found favour with Maria Theresa of Austria for whom he acted as Chamberlain. He had seven sons, the eldest was Count Walsh de Serrant whose family survive in France to the present day.

Captain Oliver Walsh, the tenth and youngest son of John Walsh (1720–1785) of Ballymountain, County Kilkenny, served in the British navy and was at the battles of Copenhagen, the Nile and Trafalgar where he was one of Nelson's youngest captains. In 1813, when only thirty-six, he died of yellow fever.

At home, in literature, Louis Walsh (1880–1942) of County Derry, was a solicitor and a District Justice of his native County Donegal. He wrote *The Life of John Mitchel*, some plays and memoirs.

Maurice Walsh (1879–1964) was one of the best-loved novelists. Born in Kerry, he started work in Scotland in the Customs and Excise. From this experience he developed a rich vein of story-telling of which *The Key Above The Door* was one of the most popular and best-selling novels for a decade. He returned to Ireland and wrote many more books, including *The Quiet Man*, which was filmed, and although some critics thought it stage-Irish, it contributed considerably to Irish tourism for it featured the magnificent scenery of the west of Ireland.

Like so many other Irish families, the famine and hard times at home drove the Walshes to seek the hospitality and opportunity of America. Robert Walsh (1784–1859) went rather earlier than most others. He was born in Baltimore, County Cork, the son of a comfortable aristocratic family who, it is supposed, had also had connections with France. He read law and worked for a while as a journalist. He was on the Federalist side in the War of Independence. He could afford to travel extensively and to be a littérateur and when he finally settled in Paris his was the first of the American salons.

Thomas James Walsh (1859–1933), a senator from Montana, was the son of Irish parents. He followed a legal career and made his reputation in copper litigation.

Michael Walsh (1815–1859) was born near Cork and was brought to America by his parents. He worked in New York as a reporter and attempted to publish a paper of his own. He got the young working men of New York city to join the Spartan Association. His aim was to destroy the hold of Tammany Hall by showing the real principles of democracy. Twice he was imprisoned for his, seemingly, anti-establishment ideas—he wrote bitingly of the squalor and the poverty he saw in New York.

Thomas Walsh (1871–1928) of Brooklyn was a complete contrast. A son of County Longford gentry, his interests were literature, particularly that of Spain. He was an accomplished pianist, a painter and a lecturer. He was also philanthropical and he is regarded as having contributed to Catholic culture, particularly by his writings on Spanish literature.

Blanche Walsh (1873–1915) was the daughter of an Irish saloon-keeper, who was also a Tammany Hall politician. She was one of the most popular actresses of her time and played most of the leading roles in the contemporary theatre, including Little Billy in *Trilby*.

In *Burke's Landed Gentry* of 1958 there are a number of different Walsh families with mention of their seats. Walshes occupy several pages in the Irish telephone directory, both in Dublin city and in all the provinces.

157

WOULFE (Wolfe)

FATHER Patrick Woulfe (d.1933), the Gaelic scholar who wrote *Sloinnte Gaedeal is Gall*, an Irish/English dictionary of Irish surnames and their origins, writes, 'Ulf, Wulf, Woulfe, Wofe son of Ulf, is a common personal name among all Teutonic races. As a surname, like so many others, it came to Ireland about the time of the Anglo-Norman invasion and is found in early Dublin rolls. Wolf,' he writes, 'is descriptive of one of a rapacious disposition.'

A branch of the Woulfe family lived in a district called Crioch Bhulbhach near the town of Monasterevan, County Kildare. The records show that the Woulfes of Limerick took an active part in the affairs of that city from the fourteenth to the middle of the sixteenth century. In 1651, when he took Limerick, Ireton exempted from pardon a Father Francis Woulfe and a Captain George Woulfe. This George Woulfe was the great-grandfather of General James Woulfe (1727–1759), the hero of Quebec.

During the reign of Queen Elizabeth, David Wolfe of Limerick was sent to Rome to study. With Ignatius od Loyola and Francis Borgia as contemporaries, he was ordained a Jesuit and was sent back to Ireland in 1560 by the Pope as an Apostolic Legate to look after the Roman Catholic Church in Ireland, to establish schools, to regulate public worship and to keep lines of communication open with the Catholic princes—a challenging assignment in those days when a priest went about at the peril of his life.

Eventually he was arrested and for a number of years he suffered rigorous imprisonment in Dublin Castle. He managed to escape to Spain but he was soon back again, faithfully carrying on his vocation. When the continual wars made it impossible for him to fulfil his duties he took refuge in a castle in Connacht. Scrupling to share their food with its occupants when he discovered they had got it by plunder, he sickened and died about the year 1578. Father David Woulfe has left an interesting description of Ireland at that time.

In the seventeenth century, because they sided with the Geraldines, the Woulfes were transplanted to Connacht—a Patrick, John and David Woulfe are mentioned specifically.

The Woulfes from Ireland were prominent in France at the time of the French Revolution, both in the church and army.

Peter Woulfe (1727?–1803), a chemist and mineralogist of Irish origin discovered native tin in Cornwall in 1766. He invented an apparatus for passing gases through liquids which became known as Woulfe's Bottle.

Stephen Woulfe (1787–1840), an Irish judge of Ennis, was of the Woulfe family that settled in County Limerick as far back as the fifteenth century. They remained staunch Roman Catholics and he was one of the earliest Roman Catholic students to gain admission to Trinity College, Dublin. He studied for the Bar and became a good advocate taking an active part in Irish politics. He made himself remarkable by withstanding Daniel O'Connell, mainly in regard to the securities which were demanded as the corollary of Catholic emancipation. Stephen Woulfe was appointed Crown Counsel of Munster and made Chief Baron of the Irish Exchequer, being the first Roman Catholic to be so appointed.

158

Arthur Wolfe, Viscount Kilwarden (1739–1803)

Arthur Wolfe (1739–1803) was the son of John Wolfe of Forenaughts, also called Furness, in County Kildare. His portrait hangs in the dining-hall of Trinity College, Dublin, where he was Vice Chancellor in 1802. He was a Chief Justice of the King's Bench and for his support of the Union he was raised to the peerage as Viscount Kilwarden. He was not thought to be a great lawyer but he had a noble and humane disposition. He showed this when he refused to strain the law against those tried before him for taking part in the insurrection of 1798, and he displayed spirit on the occasion of Wolfe Tone's trial by court-martial.

The reaction against the death on the scaffold of the young rebel, Robert Emmet, on 23rd of July 1803 was very deeply felt. That evening, Viscount Kilwarden, with his daughter and nephew, drove into Dublin on their way to a gathering at the Castle. Nearby, in Thomas Street, his carriage was stopped, and a pike was plunged into his body. His nephew was killed outright and his daughter managed to escape. As Kilwarden lay dying some officers swore they would hang those they had taken prisoners on the spot. With his last breath Kilwarden admonished them, 'Murder must be punished, but let no man suffer for my death but on a fair trial and by the laws of his country.' Barrington wrote of him: 'He had not an error to counterbalance which some merit did not exhibit itself.' Descendants of the Wolfe family still live at Furness in County Kildare.

The Reverend Charles Wolfe (1791–1823), a relative of Viscount Kilwarden, was one of eleven children, the youngest of eight sons. His father died when he was very young and his mother managed to get him an excellent education at

159

Winchester and Dublin University where he took orders. He spent the rest of his short life as curate of Donaghmore, County Down.

A man of singularly spiritual and feeling nature, it was said of him: 'In the lottery of literature, Charles Wolfe has been one of the few who have drawn the prize of probable immortality from a casual gleam of inspiration thrown over a single poem consisting of only a few stanzas.' The poem, penned in 1814, inspired by a passage written by Southey in the Edinburgh Annual Register, was *The Burial of Sir John Moore*. Charles Wolfe, completely devoted to his clerical duties, thought little of his poetry and was unperturbed at the attribution of his poem to many of the leading poets of the day. Byron first noticed the poem in 1822 and was most enthusiastic about it. Wolfe, who neglected himself utterly, died of consumption on the way to France in the care of his sisters. After his death, a letter preserved in the Royal Irish Academy showed absolute proof that Charles Wolfe was the writer of the poem. It was also discovered from his papers that, had his life span been extended, he would probably have taken his place among the foremost poets of his day.

Maurice Wolfe (d.1915), of Cratloe, Athea, County Limerick, went to America to join the U.S. Army and saw much service there during the civil war in which a very large number of Irishmen took part. All during his service he wrote letters home. He made friends with the American Indians and got a pony from them in return for a burning glass. He describes how 'The Redskins capture and burn the mails which might account for any delay in communications with home!' He sent presents home; moccasins for his mother and an Indian scalp for his brother! During the French war against Prussia, he wrote that the Irish were in sympathy with the French. These letters, written between 1863 and 1874, were published in 1957 in *The Irish Sword*, the magazine of the Irish Military History Society.

BARRY

BLAKE

BEIRNE

BOYLE

BROWNE
(Galway)

O BRIEN

BURKE

BUTLER

O BYRNE

MacCABE

MacCARTHY

O CONNELL

O CONNOR
(Kerry)

O CONNOR
(Don)

O CONNOR
(of Corcomroe)

O DALY

DILLON

O DONOGHUE

O DONNELL

O DONOVAN

DUFFY

DOYLE

FITZGERALD

O FLAHERTY

O GRADY

HELY
(Hely quartering from
the Arms of Hely-Hutchinson,
Earl of Donoghmore)

GUINNESS

HENNESSY

O KEEFFE

KAVANAGH

KELLY

KENNEDY

KEOGH

LYNCH

MacMAHON
(Oriel)

O MALLEY

MacMAHON
(Thomond)

MARTIN, MacLYSAGHT

MORE

MURPHY
(Morchoe)

MURPHY
(Muskerry)

MacNAMARA

O NEILL

NUGENT

PLUNKETT

O REILLY

POWER

SHERIDAN

O ROURKE

O SULLIVAN

O SULLIVAN
(Beare)

TAAFFE

O TOOLE

WALSH

WOULFE